KNOW
YOUR ENGLISH

VOLUME 1

SECOND EDITION

KNOW YOUR ENGLISH

VOLUME 1

IDIOMS AND THEIR STORIES

SECOND EDITION

S Upendran

Universities Press

KNOW YOUR ENGLISH, VOLUME 1, SECOND EDITION

UNIVERSITIES PRESS (INDIA) PRIVATE LIMITED

Registered Office
3-6-747/1/A & 3-6-754/1, Himayatnagar, Hyderabad 500 029, Telangana, India
info@universitiespress.com; www.universitiespress.com

Distributed by
Orient Blackswan Private Limited

Registered Office
3-6-752 Himayatnagar, Hyderabad 500 029 Telangana, India

Other Offices
Bengaluru / Chennai / Guwahati / Hyderabad / Kolkata
Mumbai / New Delhi / Noida / Patna / Visakhapatnam

First Edition 2011
Reprinted 2011 (twice), 2015, 2017

501826

Cover and book design

Illustrations
Arijit Dutta Chowdhury

ISBN 978 93 86235 60 2

Typeset in Adobe Garamond Pro BT 11.5/13.5 *by*
Orient BlackSwan

Printed in India by
SS Colour Impression Pvt Ltd, Chennai 600 106

Published by
Universities Press (India) Private Limited
3-6-747/1/A & 3-6-754/1, Himayatnagar, Hyderabad 500 029, Telangana, India

Preface to the Second Edition

'Idiom' comes from the Latin 'idios', meaning 'peculiar', and according to a rough estimate, there are over twenty thousand idiomatic expressions in English. For second language learners, learning these peculiar expressions poses a great challenge for there is no one-to-one correspondence between the words that make up an idiom and its meaning. Why is a nutritious meal, for example, often referred to as a 'square meal' instead of a 'round' or a 'rectangular' one? What is the connection between someone who daydreams and 'wool gathering'?

This book is an enlarged edition of the slim volume that was brought out in 2011. The 570 idioms and other everyday expressions included in this edition are selections from the weekly column, *Know Your English*, published in *The Hindu*. The entries have been arranged alphabetically, and each provides the meaning of the idiom along with its possible origin. Examples have been provided to illustrate how the expression is used in everyday contexts. Where several theories exist to explain the origin of an idiom, I have included the one that is most likely to help the reader recall the meaning – even though scholars may have rubbished the probable theory. Explanations, as far as possible, have been provided in simple language.

I am grateful to the Editor of *The Hindu* for giving me permission to use the material from the column. Heartfelt thanks are also due to the members of my family and friends who have offered valuable suggestions, advice and help. I would also like to thank the readers of the column for their letters of appreciation and condemnation. Last, but not least, I would like to thank my father, K. Subrahmanian, who began writing the *Know Your English* column nearly 40 years ago. This book would not have been possible without him.

S. Upendran

To My Father

Contents

A lick and a promise

Meaning to do a job in a careless and hurried manner; to do something half-heartedly.

Examples After working all day in the garden, I was too tired to dust the furniture. But my mother insisted that I do it. So, I gave it a lick and a promise and went to bed.

Every morning I put on my uniform, give my shoes a lick and a promise and rush to school.

Origin In informal contexts, the word 'lick' means 'a hasty wash'. Therefore, in the context of the idiom, the word is used to mean 'hasty'. The 'promise' refers to the assurance that the worker(s) will do a thorough job sometime later.

Above board

Meaning an honest deal; no trickery involved.

Examples If politicians were involved, you can be pretty sure that not everything was above board.

Raju is straight as they come. All his dealings are above board.

Origin According to some scholars, the 'board' in this expression refers to a table. An 'above board' deal is one that is done in an open manner – the hands of the participants involved are out in the open for everyone to see. There is no underhand dealing involved.

Another explanation has to do with the smuggling of goods on ships. In the old days, people who smuggled things hid the contraband items below deck. Legal cargo, on the other hand, was placed in plain sight on the deck. In other words, anything that was placed on the deck was 'above board'!

Achilles' heel

Meaning an individual's weakness; something that other people can attack or take advantage of.

Examples Rohini's Achilles' heel is pressure. She just can't handle it.

Udita's vanity is her Achilles' heel.

Origin Achilles was a famous Greek warrior. As soon as he was born, his mother, Thetis, dipped him in the river Styx in order to make him invincible. Legend had it that no harm would come to a person who had been dipped in the river. Unfortunately for Achilles, when his mother immersed him, she held him by the heel. As a result, the water never touched this portion of his foot; the heel became Achilles' weak spot. He died in the Trojan War when an arrow pierced his heel.

Pronunciation The 'a' is like the 'a' in 'china', while the following 'ch' is like the 'k' in 'kiss' and 'kite'. The 'i' sounds like the 'i' in 'it' and 'kit'; the final 'e' is like the 'ee' in 'peel' and 'feel'. The 's' sounds like the 'z' in 'zip'. The name is pronounced 'a-**KI**-leez', with the stress on the second syllable.

Across the board

Meaning a rule or a policy that will affect everyone; something that will be applied uniformly.

These human beings are crazy. How am I supposed to come first, second and third in the same race?

Examples — The Chairman said there would be a salary increase across the board.

Public sector units should aim at increasing productivity across the board.

Origin — The expression comes from the world of horse racing. The 'board' refers to the blackboard on which bookmakers wrote the odds for every horse in each race. If you place a bet on a horse across the board, what you are doing is placing an equal amount of money on the animal coming first, second or third. If you bet ₹100 on the horse coming first, you wager a similar amount on the same horse coming second or third as well. You are selecting all three options.

Adam's ale

Meaning — water.

Examples — Would you like to wash down the sandwich with Adam's ale?

I don't have any soft drinks. Would you be interested in Adam's ale?

Origin — The only drink that Adam and Eve had available to them was water.

Adam's apple

Meaning — the protrusion of the thyroid cartilage in a man's neck is usually referred to as Adam's apple. One can see it move up and down when the individual tries to swallow something.

Example — You can't miss Vijay. He's the man with the enormous Adam's apple.

Origin — It is based on the story of Adam and Eve. After tasting the forbidden fruit, Eve asks her partner to take a bite. Adam obliges, and the apple gets stuck in his throat!

Add insult to injury

Meaning — to make a situation that is already bad, worse.

Examples — Ashish was driving on the wrong side of the road when he hit my car. To add insult to injury, he abused me for driving slowly!

Rohan was given out when he was definitely not out. To add insult to injury, he was fined 50% of his match fee for showing dissent.

Origin — The expression comes from a story in *Aesop's Fables* in which a bald man tries to swat a fly that has landed on his head. He misses the fly and smacks his own head instead. The fly tells the man, "You wanted to kill me for a mere touch.

What will you do to yourself, now that you have added insult to injury?"

Albatross around the neck

Meaning a burden; a sense of guilt which becomes an obstacle to someone's success.

Examples The failed project has become an albatross around Sunila's neck. Her boss rejects all her new proposals without even looking at them.

According to my mother, the old car is an albatross around my father's neck.

Origin An albatross is a large bird which is found at sea. Sailors believe that killing this bird brings bad luck. Samuel Taylor Coleridge's poem, *The Rime of the Ancient Mariner*, written in 1798, tells the story of a sailor who kills an albatross. As soon as the bird is killed, things go terribly wrong on the ship: the wind dies, and the crew runs out of drinking water. The sailor's angry shipmates hang the dead bird around his neck as a sign of his guilt.

All ears

Meaning eager to listen to what someone has to say.

Examples Tell me everything that happened at the party. I'm all ears.

When the physics teacher read out our marks, we were all ears.

Origin — When you say you are all ears, you are implying that the other senses are almost non-existent. Your ears alone are fully functional; you are, therefore, eager to hear what someone has to say.

All hell broke loose

Meaning — pandemonium; a situation that is completely out of control.

Examples — When the students were told that their demands would not be met, all hell broke loose.

All hell broke loose when Lavanya saw the article in the magazine.

Origin — The expression comes from Milton's *Paradise Lost*. Before he is thrown out of the Garden of Eden, Satan meets Gabriel, an angel who acts as a messenger from God. Gabriel asks the Devil: "Wherefore with thee / Came not all hell broke loose?"

All thumbs

Meaning — to be very clumsy and awkward when it comes to working with one's hands.

Examples I never ask Govind to dust those expensive vases. He's all thumbs.

I asked Priya to thread the needle, but she couldn't. She's all thumbs today.

Origin If all your fingers were thumbs, you would be unable to do many of the things you can do now.

Always a bridesmaid and never a bride

Meaning to never fulfill your ambition; always second best.

Examples My cousin took part in the elections, and lost again. She is always a bridesmaid, never a bride.

My friend Rachel is a wonderful actor. But unfortunately, she's always a bridesmaid, and never a bride.

Origin Unlike a bride, the bridesmaid is never the focus of attention.

American dream

Meaning to lead a life of success.

Examples The young couple from China is living the American dream.

The American dream is not easy to achieve. You need to work really hard.

Origin — The term was coined by James Truslow Adams in his book, *Epic of America*, written in 1931. In it, he wrote: "The American Dream is that dream of a land in which life should be better and richer and fuller for everyone, with opportunity for each according to ability or achievement."

(the) Apple doesn't fall far from the tree

Meaning — a rather old saying which means that children grow up to be like their parents. Idioms which have more or less the same meaning are 'chip off the old block' and 'like father, like son'.

Examples — Like his father, Vinod ended up becoming a politician. You know what they say, the apple doesn't fall far from the tree.

Both mother and daughter love shopping. The apple doesn't fall far from the tree.

Origin — When an apple falls from a tree, it falls under it or some place very close to it.

Apple of discord

Meaning — something which is a cause of dispute; a bone of contention.

Examples The right to host the one-day international has become the apple of discord between the two states.

The new computer has become the apple of discord between the twins.

Origin According to legend, when Thetis and Peleus got married, they invited all the Greek gods, except the God of Discord, Eris, to their wedding. Makes sense, doesn't it? Nobody wants a disagreement or a quarrel during a wedding. Eris was so angry she had not been invited, she decided to spoil the event by tossing a golden apple among the guests. On the apple were written three words: 'For the fairest'. Three goddesses, Hera, Athene and Aphrodite, fought for the apple because each believed that she was the fairest of them all. They asked Paris, the Prince of Troy, to decide the matter for them. Each goddess tried to bribe Paris into giving her the apple. Hera promised him all of Asia, while Athene promised him glory in war. Aphrodite, the Goddess of Love, promised him the most beautiful woman in the world; a woman whose face was capable of launching a thousand ships. Young Paris gave the apple to Aphrodite, and he got the beautiful Helen in return. Hera and Athene, as expected, were extremely angry with Paris and they plotted his ruin: they ensured that the beautiful city of Troy was destroyed.

Apple of one's eye

Meaning a prized possession; an object or person which/whom you like and look after with a great deal of devotion.

Examples Anita is the apple of her father's eye.

Don't say anything nasty about that painting. It's the apple of Seema's eye.

Origin The 'apple' here does not refer to the fruit, but the 'pupil' in one's eye. People felt that the shape of the pupil was similar to the shape of an apple. In fact, for quite some time, the word 'aeppel' was used to refer to both the eye and the fruit. The pupil is a priceless possession, for without it, we would be unable to see. Since vision is something that all human beings value, the expression 'apple of one's eye' came to mean 'something that is greatly valued or treasured'.

Apple-pie order

Meaning in perfect order; when everything has been neatly arranged and things are in their proper place.

Examples This room is a mess. By the time I return, I want everything to be in apple-pie order.

Rashmi keeps her belongings in apple-pie order.

Origin Scholars believe the idiom is a corruption of the French 'nappe plié', meaning 'folded linen'. Some people, however, believe that it was a Colonial (that is what Americans were called before they got their independence) housewife living in New England who made the idiom popular. The story goes that this lady was in the habit of baking seven apple pies every Sunday – one pie for every day of the coming week. Once the pies had been baked and cooled, she proceeded to place them on different shelves. The pie that was to be eaten on Monday was placed on the first shelf, the one to be eaten on Tuesday on the shelf next to it, and so on. The lady was so meticulous that she made sure that all the pies were lined up just right.

Argus-eyed

Meaning to be watchful, vigilant.

Examples The police were watching the proceedings, Argus-eyed.

The students found it difficult to get past the Argus-eyed watchman.

Origin Argus was a giant who had fifty pairs of eyes. Juno, wife of Jupiter, asked him to keep an eye on her heifer (young cow), Io. The vigilant Argus stood guard, and when he felt drowsy, he allowed only two of his eyes to close. The remaining forty-nine pairs of eyes were focused on Io. Unfortunately for the giant, the messenger of the gods, Mercury, became interested in the heifer and decided to steal it. In order to achieve this, he began playing his lyre. The music was so soothing that Argus fell asleep – all one hundred eyes closed. Mercury drew his sword and promptly chopped off the giant's head. When Juno saw what had happened, she removed the eyes from the head of the giant and placed them all on the tail of a peacock. This explains why we talk about the eye on a peacock's feather.

Armchair critic

Meaning someone who has become knowledgeable by reading, sitting in his favourite armchair; a person with little or no practical experience.

Examples If you want words of wisdom from an armchair critic, you can go to Laxman.

I want someone who has dealt with this problem, not some armchair critic.

Origin The origin is fairly obvious. It was in the late 19th century that the expression began to mean, 'criticism of matters in which the critic takes no active part'.

Arms of Morpheus

Meaning sound asleep.

Examples Jadeja was in the arms of Morpheus when the telephone rang.

Anamika has been in the arms of Morpheus all day.

Origin Morpheus is the God of dreams in Roman and Greek mythology. So, when you are in his arms, you are in the land of dreams. It is from this name that we get the word 'morphine'.

Ask for the moon

Meaning to ask for something impossible.

Examples The new teacher wants her students to come to class on time. Frankly, she is asking for the moon.

My neighbour wants her husband to go on a diet and lose about twenty pounds. I think she is asking for the moon.

Origin It is like a small child asking her parents for the moon.

Asleep at the switch

Meaning failing to do one's job competently.

Examples The dacoits managed to break into the house because the watchman was asleep at the switch.

According to Richard Clark, 9/11 happened because President Bush and his team were asleep at the switch.

Origin When you journey from one place to another by train, the locomotive often changes tracks. In the 19th century, in the United States, tracks were changed manually by pulling upon a lever. If the person whose responsibility it was to change tracks fell asleep on the job, it resulted in an accident.

At the helm

Meaning usually used to refer to a leader or someone who is in charge of something.

Examples The company is doomed. The Board has decided that Sashi will be at the helm.

Prema has been requested to be at the helm till she retires in July.

Origin Drivers make use of the steering wheel to steer a vehicle in a particular direction. In the case of a boat or a ship, it is the 'helm' that functions as a steering wheel. The person who is 'at the helm' is referred to as the 'helmsman'. He determines in which direction the ship will go.

Axe to grind

Meaning to do or say something with an ulterior motive in mind; to complain about something.

Examples Why is Sachi being so helpful all of a sudden? I think she has an axe to grind.

Maurya wants to talk to you. I'm sure he has an axe to grind.

Origin According to some scholars, the expression comes from a story written by Charles Miner in 1810. In the story, a boy is sitting next to a grindstone – a tool used to sharpen metals. A stranger carrying a blunt axe flatters the boy, and then proceeds to ask him how the grindstone works. The boy shows him how it works by sharpening the man's axe for him; the stranger, having duped the boy, walks away laughing. Many attribute this story to Benjamin Franklin.

Back to square one

Meaning to go back to the beginning and start all over again; to return to the starting point.

Examples After three days of house hunting, I found one I really liked. A few days later, when I went to pay the advance, I realised someone had already moved in. So, it was back to square one.

My boss didn't like any of the designs we'd given him. It's back to square one.

Origin The expression was made popular by sports commentators of the BBC. Since football is a game that is difficult to follow on the radio, some enterprising radio commentators in the early 20th century divided the field into eight squares. The commentators informed the audience of what was happening on the field by telling them which square the ball was in. On the day of the game, most newspapers and sports magazines carried a drawing of the playing field with the squares clearly marked and numbered – this made it easy for listeners to follow the action. Square one was where the goalie stood. Others believe that the idiom has its origins in board games like Snakes and Ladders.

Bad egg

Meaning a dishonest and unreliable person; reprehensible character.

Examples In our movies, it's usually the policeman who is a bad egg.

Tell your students to stay away from Sridhar. He's a bad egg.

Origin When you call someone a 'bad egg', you are saying he is a horrible person; he stinks like an egg that has gone bad.

Badger someone

Meaning to pester someone; when you 'badger someone into doing something', you keep annoying or bothering the person till he becomes frustrated and agrees to do what you want him to.

Examples The children badgered their father into taking them to a movie.

Anita kept badgering her father to let him cut her hair short.

Origin The idiom comes from the cruel sport of badger baiting. In this game, dogs were turned loose on a badger, a furry animal, placed in an empty barrel or a hole. When the vicious dogs managed to drag the frightened animal out, the hounds and the badger were separated. The injured animal was put back in the barrel or hole, and the cruel process was repeated till the poor badger had been ripped to pieces.

Baker's dozen

Meaning thirteen.

Examples How many loaves do we need? I'd say a baker's dozen.

Don't give me just ten roses. Give me a baker's dozen.

Origin In 1266, in England, a law was passed in Parliament which specified exactly how much a loaf of bread should weigh. When a baker sold a loaf that was less than the specified weight, a heavy penalty was imposed on him. To prevent this from happening, a baker always gave an extra loaf to the customer. If you bought 12 loaves of bread, the baker gave you 13 just to make sure he was not penalised.

Bald as a coot

Meaning to be completely bald.

Examples My neighbour is as bald as a coot.

My twenty-five-year-old cousin is as bald as a coot. We've been telling him to wear a wig.

Origin A 'coot' is a small, dark bird which has a white patch on its head. It is not bald; it has feathers on its head. One of the meanings of the word 'bald' is 'marked with white'. It is because of the white spot on the bird's head that we get the expression 'bald as a coot'.

Banana republic

Meaning originally, a small country in Central/South America where there was political instability.

Nowadays, the term is used to refer to any country which is in constant political turmoil.

Examples You can't do whatever you want in this country. This is no banana republic.

Our CEO is planning to visit one of those banana republics next month.

Origin Many of the poor countries in South America were derisively called banana republics because the banana was the only thing they exported: the fruit was their main source of income. The governments in these countries were very weak, and coups were common.

Band-aid solution

Meaning a temporary solution to a problem.

Examples Our politicians always come up with band-aid solutions to our water problem.

When I told Narender about the predicament I was in, he gave me a band-aid solution.

Origin A band-aid is something that we put on small cuts. If the cut or injury is major, the band-aid will be of no help.

Bark up the wrong tree

Meaning to make the wrong choice or follow the wrong course of action.

Examples If you think you are going to get Sonia's job by being nice to the Chairman, you are barking up the wrong tree.

The players blamed Azhar for their problems, but they were barking up the wrong tree.

Origin The expression comes from the sport of raccoon hunting. A raccoon (also spelt racoon) is a small furry animal found mostly in North America. These animals, being nocturnal, are hunted at night. In order to catch them, hunters make use of dogs. The dogs chase these animals and drive them up a tree. Once a raccoon is driven up a tree, the dogs stand under it and keep barking. This is their way of telling their masters that there is an animal hiding in the tree. Sometimes, of course, the dogs pick the wrong tree to bark at – one in which there is no raccoon.

Barkis is willing

Meaning to indicate one's willingness or readiness to do something.

Examples If she is willing to go, tell her that Barkis is willing.

That sounds like a wonderful trip. Barkis is willing.

Origin The expression first appeared in Charles Dickens' well-known classic, *David Copperfield*. Barkis is the name of one of the characters in the novel. He keeps sending a message through David to Clara Peggotty, the maid of David's mother. The message that David is to give Clara is "Barkis is willing". In other words, Barkis is willing to marry Clara.

Bat an eyelid

Meaning to show no surprise or concern. Usually used in the negative.

Examples When Gupta heard the terrible news, he didn't bat an eyelid.

When my cousin was told he had won the lottery, he didn't bat an eyelid.

Origin The word 'bat' in this context means 'to open and shut one's eyes quickly'. When people receive shocking or surprising news, they tend to bat their eyelids. If one does not bat them, it shows that the person is not surprised or shocked by what he has heard.

Be on one's high horse

Meaning to behave in a proud and arrogant manner; to treat others with utter contempt because you think you are morally superior to them.

Examples A lot of people think it's about time Chandu got off his high horse.

Whatever you do, don't get on your high horse and refuse to answer questions.

Origin In England, in the old days, a person's rank was determined by the height of the horse he rode. If you were a nobleman or a person of some importance, you invariably rode a 'high horse'. These horses were usually much taller than the horses ridden by the common man. Riding such high or tall horses began to be equated with superiority.

Be-all and end-all

Meaning mostly used in informal contexts to mean 'the most important thing or the only thing that matters'.

Examples Vinita's adopted children have become the be-all and end-all of her existence.

My uncle believes that profit should not become the be-all and end-all of business.

Origin Shakespeare is believed to have coined this expression in his tragedy, *Macbeth*. The hero, Macbeth, realises that the only way he can become the King of Scotland is by killing Duncan. Macbeth says, "That but this blow might be the be-all and the end-all".

Beat around the bush

Meaning not getting to the point; answering questions in an indirect manner to conceal one's real intentions. It is also possible to say 'beat about the bush'.

Examples For God's sake, stop beating about/around the bush. How much is it going to cost?

Will you please stop beating around/about the bush? Just answer my question.

Origin In the cruel sport of 'batfowling', people ('batfowlers') entered the forest during the night and proceeded to kill 'fowls' (birds) with the 'bats' or clubs they were carrying. The batfowlers and their servants used to scare the birds by beating around the bush in which the birds were sleeping. The sleepy birds, dazed and confused by the sudden commotion, would then fly directly to the bright lights that the men were carrying. Here, they were beaten to death. The batfowlers who beat about the bush were not really interested in the bush; they were interested in the birds that were sleeping inside.

Beck and call

Meaning to do whatever a person wants you to; to remain slavishly attentive to all his needs.

Examples The young prince was at his wife's beck and call.

There are a few reporters we know who are at the Minister's beck and call.

Origin The word 'beck' is actually the shortened form of 'beckon'. A 'beck' is usually a silent signal that you give someone in order to draw his attention. The signal could be a simple nod of the head or the motioning of one's finger. Who are the people who pay a great deal of attention to someone's head and hand movements? Servants, of course! In the old days, servants were at their master's beck and call. A master could get a servant to do his bidding in two different ways – he could either 'call' the servant or 'beckon' him.

Bells and whistles

Meaning rather attractive but inessential add-on features of a gadget.

Examples You don't need the bells and whistles. They will double the cost.

Ramesh likes to buy gadgets with all the bells and whistles.

Origin This expression of American origin was made popular in the 19th century when people started moving west. Since new towns were springing up all the time, merchants travelled great distances to sell their goods. Before entering a town, the

I see that this model comes with all the bells and whistles.

merchants tied a bell to the wagon in which they were travelling. The wagon's movement made the bell ring; and as they neared the town, the merchants added to the noise by blowing on a whistle. The sound made by the bell and the whistle informed everyone in town that the merchants had arrived.

Belly up

Meaning to go bankrupt.

Examples The chit fund company went belly up within three months.

There are rumours that Dilip's company is likely to go belly up.

Origin An organisation is being compared to a dead fish. When a fish dies, it floats upside down. It goes 'belly up'.

Best (greatest) thing since sliced bread

Meaning wonderful; something that is to be appreciated very much.

Examples When cable television came to India, many thought it was the greatest thing since sliced bread.

Meera thinks the Harry Potter novels are the best thing since sliced bread.

Origin Before 1928, people could only buy unsliced bread; the slicing was done at home. When the sliced loaf was introduced, the advertisement said that it was "the greatest forward step in the baking industry since bread was wrapped." It is from this advertisement that we get the expression.

Better half

Meaning — this rather old-fashioned expression is used to refer to one's spouse – the 'better half' can be the husband or the wife!

Examples — Unlike Usha, her better half seldom has anything interesting to say.

Jim's better half has a very good sense of humour.

Origin — The expression has been around for many centuries; in fact, the first person to use it was the Roman poet, Horace. When he employed the term for the first time, he used it to refer to his friend, and not his spouse. With the passage of time, 'better half' acquired a totally different meaning. It was used to refer to an individual's soul. By the time it was borrowed into English, the term meant 'one's friend or one's lover'. It was in this sense that Sir Philip Sydney used it in his famous book, *Arcadia*. It was only years later that the term began to mean what it does today – one's spouse.

Between Scylla and Charybdis

Meaning — threatened by two dangers at the same time, and in trying to avoid one, you fall victim to the other.

Example Revathi wanted to be on good terms with her in-laws and her parents. But the effort of pleasing one without offending the other was like steering between Scylla and Charybdis.

Origin Scylla and Charybdis are the names of two rocks located in a narrow sea passage in the Straits of Messina. Scylla is located on the Italian side, while Charybdis is on the Sicilian side. In Greek mythology, Scylla was a female monster with twelve feet and six heads. She had razor sharp teeth and was capable of ripping apart sailors who had the misfortune of coming too close to her. Charybdis was a whirlpool. It was seen as a monster which gulped down huge amounts of water, and in the process sucked in sailors who accidentally got close to it. When Ulysses tried to make his way through this narrow passageway, Scylla managed to kill six of his sailors. Shakespeare used the idiom in *Merchant of Venice*: "When I shun Scylla, your father, I fall into Charybdis, your mother."

Pronunciation The 'scy' in 'Scylla' is pronounced like the 'si' in 'sit', 'sip' and 'sin', while the final 'a' is like the 'a' in 'china'. The name is pronounced '**SI**-le' with the stress on the first syllable. The 'ch' in 'Charybdis' is pronounced like the 'k' in 'kit', 'kill' and 'kiss'. The following 'a' is like the 'a' in 'china', while the 'y' and the 'i' are like the 'i' in 'kit', 'pit' and 'sit'. The name is pronounced 'ke-**RIB**-dis' with the stress on the second syllable.

Between the devil and the deep blue sea

Meaning faced with having to choose between two very unpleasant situations. The choice given is not much of a choice at all; either way, you end up doing something risky or undesirable.

Examples The villain's henchmen were close behind him, and the river in front of him was full of hungry crocodiles. Caught between the devil and the deep blue sea, Mani hesitated.

If she marries Bala, Rita knows she will be unhappy for the rest of her life. If she doesn't marry him, her parents will be angry. She is caught between the devil and the deep blue sea!

Origin If you are in a situation where you have to choose between the devil and the sea, you don't really have much of a choice, do you? Either way, your fate is sealed. Other idioms which have the same meaning are 'between Scylla and Charybdis' and 'between a rock and a hard place'.

Beyond his ken

Meaning beyond someone's understanding.

Examples Please don't talk to me about grammar. It is just beyond my ken.

Listen to me, my young friend. These complex issues are beyond your ken.

Origin The word 'ken' is Scottish in origin, and it means 'to know someone or something'. Therefore, when you say that something is 'beyond my ken', you mean you do not know anything about it for it is beyond your understanding.

Beyond the pale

Meaning behaving in an unacceptable or an uncivilised manner.

Examples Rajagopal's behaviour at the meeting was beyond the pale.

Sushmita is never invited to parties because her behaviour is considered beyond the pale.

Origin The word 'pale' has nothing to do with colour. It comes from the Latin 'pãlus', meaning 'stake'. In the old days, 'stakes' or wooden poles were used to mark the boundaries of one's territory. Everything that was within the 'pale' or the wooden fence belonged to you, and the land that was outside it belonged to someone else. The expression 'beyond the pale' began to be used in the 14th century when parts of Ireland came under the English. Territories that were 'within the pale' belonged to the English; those that were outside it, belonged to the Irish. The English, as you may expect, did not have a very good opinion of their neighbours. They thought that the Irish were crude people who did not know how to behave in a civilised manner.

Big Apple

Meaning the city of New York.

Examples Veda spent ten years in the States without ever visiting the Big Apple.

Rushika says she's fallen in love with the Big Apple.

Origin The term 'Big Apple' has been used to refer to the city of New York since the 1920s. It is believed that African-American stable boys working in the racetracks of New Orleans were the first to refer to New York as 'Big Apple'. Many of the important horse races were held in New York and it was the dream of most jockeys and boys working in stables to get there. If you managed to make it to New York, you had arrived; you had made it big. A sports reporter, John Fitzgerald, liked the term so much that he called his popular racing column, *Around the Big Apple*. In his introduction to the column on 18 February 1924, he wrote, "The Big Apple. The dream of every lad that ever threw a leg over a thoroughbred and the goal of all horsemen. There's only one Big Apple. That's New York."

Big fish in a small pond

Meaning — an individual who is important in a rather small town, organisation, etc.

Examples — Sujatha is tired of being a big fish in a small pond.

What Abhay doesn't realise is that he is a big fish in a small pond.

Origin — If you are a big fish in a small or little pond, you are seen as an important person in that small area. Outside your little world, you are a nobody.

Bigwig

Meaning — someone who holds an important or a powerful position.

Examples — We have invited some of the bigwigs for dinner.

A few of the local bigwigs are expected to be present at the meeting.

Origin — Several centuries ago, wearing wigs was a fashion in Europe. All men, whether they were bald or not, wore wigs. The richer you were, the more wigs you had. France's Louis XIV started the practice of wearing really long wigs, and soon all of Europe's royalty began to copy him. In England, the length of the wig that a man wore was dependent on his importance – or his perceived importance. The more important you were, the longer your wig was. Soon, a lot of people began to wear full-length wigs. As a result, a law was passed declaring that only nobility, judges and bishops could wear full-length wigs.

Bite the bullet

Meaning: to accept something difficult or unpleasant and endure it; to put up with a bad situation.

Examples: Rohan decided to bite the bullet and pay extra for the car that he really wanted.

Housewives are biting the bullet after another increase in the price of milk.

Origin: In the old days, there were no painkillers. When doctors operated on patients, they did not give them anaesthesia, they merely gave them something to bite on – a piece of wood, a piece of iron, etc. This was done to help the patient endure the pain, not to get rid of it. Having something in the mouth also prevented the patient from screaming into the doctor's ears! During wars, when soldiers had to be operated on, doctors usually gave them a bullet to bite on.

Bite the dust

Meaning: to die. When used with 'things', it means 'to stop working'.

Examples Most of the characters in the movie bite the dust in the first half hour.

I hope that old scooter bites the dust soon.

Origin The expression comes from Homer's *Iliad*. This is how William Cullen Bryant, an American poet, translated a few lines from the epic: "...his fellow warriors, many a one / Fall round him to the earth and bite the dust." The people who are biting the dust in this case are soldiers. When a man is slain and falls dead in a battlefield, he sometimes literally bites the dust.

Bite your tongue

Meaning asking someone to take back what they have said; to stop talking.

Examples You are accusing my brother of stealing your old car! Bite your tongue.

The suggestion given by my boss was really stupid, but I thought it wise to bite my tongue.

Origin The expression is a literal translation of the Yiddish saying, 'bays dir ditsung'. Biting your tongue will prevent you from talking. You will remain silent. Shakespeare was very fond of this expression.

Bitter end

Meaning — when you tell someone that you will be with him 'to the bitter end', you mean that you will stay with the individual to the very end. You will be with him through thick and thin, come what may. Usually, the end is rather unpleasant.

Examples — Kohli may have lost, but he fought to the bitter end.

Most people deserted Ganesh. But Sarita supported him to the bitter end.

Origin — In the early days of shipping, the anchor rope was tied to a device on the ship's bow called the 'bitt'. The portion of the rope that was tied to the 'bitt' was called the 'bitter end'. When the anchor was tossed overboard, and it reached the bitter end, it implied that there was no more rope to be 'paid out'. You had come to the very end.

Blackball

Meaning — to vote against someone joining a club.

Examples — There was a secret ballot, and poor Rahul was blackballed.

We can't allow a person like Bhaveen to join our club. We must blackball him.

Origin The expression goes back to a practice that was followed in ancient Greece. Admission to a club/ society was determined by a secret vote by all the members concerned. Each member of the club had to drop a round pebble into a box: he had to choose either a white pebble or a black pebble. When all the members had cast their vote, the box was emptied of the pebbles. If there was even one black pebble among them, the applicant was denied admission. The members had blackballed him.

Blaze a trail

Meaning to innovate; to do something that no one has done before, and which will benefit other people.

Examples The company has blazed a trail in developing new medicines for curing AIDS.

Ritu has blazed a trail in developing awareness among people about cancer.

Origin The expression came into being in the late 18th century when American settlers were pushing further and further west – towards Oregon, California, etc. Since they were exploring uncharted territory, they used to mark the trail they had taken. One method they adopted to keep track of the route was to remove the bark from some of the trees. This method of marking trees was known as 'blazing'. It is from this act of marking a trail that we get the two expressions 'blaze a trail' and 'trail blazer'.

Blow one's own trumpet/horn

Meaning praise oneself; brag or boast about one's achievements. It is also possible to say, 'to toot one's own horn'.

Examples I won't do it. I don't want people to think I'm blowing my own trumpet.

It is common for politicians to toot their own horns.

Origin In the old days, the arrival of a king or someone of importance was announced by the blowing of trumpets. When the trumpets sounded, all conversations stopped; they got the attention of all those present. If someone blows his own trumpet, he is trying to get the attention of others by praising himself.

Blue blood

Meaning a person of high or noble birth.

Examples Do you know that Saurabh is a blue-blooded aristocrat?

Don't be crazy. There's no blue blood running in Devika's veins.

Origin The term 'blue blood' is actually a translation of the Spanish, 'sangre azul'. At one time, the Moors (people of the Arab race) ruled over much of Spain. The Moors were dark complexioned and during the seven centuries they ruled Spain, a lot of interracial marriages took place. But the Spanish aristocrats who lived in Castile did not intermarry with the Moors. As a result, they remained extremely fair, and began to distinguish themselves from their rulers and fellow aristocrats by calling themselves 'sangre azul'. They meant that because of their very fair complexion, the veins in their arms looked blue. It was as if blue blood was running in their veins. The term was borrowed by other European countries to describe a nobleman. In England, the expression was borrowed to refer to prestigious institutions as well. Oxford and Cambridge, for example, are called 'blue brick' universities.

Blue-eyed boy/girl

Meaning a young man/woman who receives special treatment by those in power; the individual is admired by his/her bosses and, being their favourite, is often groomed to become a leader. It is a rather old expression that is mostly used in British and Australian English to show disapproval. The Americans prefer to say 'fair-haired boy/girl'.

Examples Bala was never the blue-eyed/fair-haired boy of the administration.

Ritu, the blue-eyed/fair-haired girl of the media, was present at the meeting.

Origin In western mythology, the hero was always 'fair'; he usually had light-coloured hair (blond) and blue eyes. The villain, on the other hand, was dark complexioned (when compared to the 'god-like' hero) and had dark hair.

Bolt from the blue

Meaning sudden and totally unexpected. Also possible to say, 'bolt out of the blue'.

Examples The news that Sumithra had lung cancer was a bolt from the blue.

When we heard that Vijaya was going to marry Hemant, it was a bolt out of the blue.

Origin The word 'blue' in the expression refers to the blue sky, and 'bolt' to thunderbolts. On a day when the sky is blue and there are no clouds around, you do not expect to hear thunder. If you do, you are really surprised.

Bone of contention

Meaning something that causes dissension; a source of trouble.

Examples If the two girls have to share the car, then it's going to become a bone of contention.

The dam has always been a bone of contention between the two countries.

Origin When people belonging to two groups get together, they often have arguments, which lead to unpleasant situations. They are like dogs fighting over a single piece of bone. The idiom has more or less the same meaning as 'apple of discord'.

Boot is on the other foot

Meaning the situation is the opposite of what it was earlier; the tables have turned. Americans tend to say, 'the shoe is on the other foot'.

Examples When they were children, they did what we told them to. The shoe is on the other foot now.

The Americans are realising that they can't get other countries to do what they want them to. The boot is on the other foot now.

Origin Nowadays, when we buy a pair of shoes or boots, we know which one is to be worn on the left foot and which is to be worn on the right. Before the 18th century, however, the idea of having a shoe specially designed for a particular foot did not exist. The shoes/boots made those days were designed to fit either foot. You could wear the same boot on your left or right leg. The shoe that you chose to wear on your left foot yesterday may be on your other foot (right) today!

Born in the purple

Meaning a child born to a prominent couple. Some people prefer to say, 'born to the purple'.

Examples Umesh was born in the purple. It is not surprising, therefore, that the media have spent the last five years watching his every move.

The hero was born in the purple. The heroine comes from a middle-class family.

Origin This rather old expression was originally used to refer to babies born to members of the royal family. The room in which a queen gave birth was usually completely covered in purple. Later, the expression included not just children of royalty, but also the children of aristocrats and high-ranking officials. The word 'purple' comes from the Greek 'porphyra'. It referred to a kind of shellfish that yielded purple dye. The Phoenicians extracted small quantities of this rather expensive dye in the city of Tyre. Since it was expensive and very few people could afford it, kings chose to make 'Tyrian purple', the colour of royalty. They passed laws that ensured that no other member of society could wear clothes of this colour.

Born with a silver spoon in the mouth

Meaning to be born into a very rich family; born with many advantages.

Examples You can't compete with Priyanca. She was born with a silver spoon in her mouth.

People who went to that school were born with a silver spoon in their mouth.

Origin In the old days, when a child was born, it was customary for the godparents to present spoons during the christening ceremony. If the godparents were well-to-do, they usually gave their godchild a silver spoon.

Boxing Day

Meaning 26 December.

Examples Why don't we go trekking on Boxing Day?

The Australians always play a test match on Boxing Day.

Origin The expression has nothing to do with the sport of boxing. Special boxes were placed inside churches in which people deposited money throughout the year. The boxes were opened the day after Christmas (26 December), and the money collected was distributed among the poor.

Bread and butter

Meaning an activity which provides the main source of income.

Examples Comedies and musicals are the bread and butter of the local theatre.

Films and film songs are the bread and butter of cable television networks.

Origin In the old days, both the rich and the poor ate bread and butter. For the poor, it was their staple diet, as it was one of the few things they could afford.

Bread-and-butter letter

Meaning a thank you letter.

Examples I was quite surprised to receive a bread-and-butter letter from my uncle.

I'd like you to sit down and write a bread-and-butter letter to them.

Origin In the old days, whenever you spent a couple of days at someone's house as a guest, you usually wrote them a letter thanking them for their hospitality. This was called a 'bread-and-butter letter'. Considering the fact that snail mail has gone out of fashion, do not be surprised if the use of this idiom goes out of fashion as well.

Maybe the idiom should be changed to 'bread-and-butter email' or 'bread-and-butter call'.

Break a leg

Meaning used mostly in the world of theatre to mean 'good luck'. This manner of wishing people is used in other contexts as well.

Examples I heard you are trying out for the band. Break a leg.

When Roshni auditioned for the lead in *Sakunthala*, I told her to break a leg.

Origin According to one theory, people who worked in theatre were a superstitious lot; they believed the evil spirits that haunted every theatre took delight in ruining every play that was staged. So, when you wished an actor 'good luck', the spirits ensured that bad luck fell upon him. In order to outwit the spirits, theatre professionals began to wish actors ill luck, like breaking a leg, rather than good luck.

Break the ice

Meaning trying to start a conversation by putting the other person at ease.

Examples Ashwini is very outgoing. She is always the first to break the ice at parties.

Sriraman attempted to break the ice by suggesting that we all play cricket.

Origin The expression comes from the world of sailing. In the old days, when sailors were ordered to break the ice, they did exactly that. During winter, when rivers froze, sailors often had to get off their ships and use an axe to break the ice so that their ship could sail through. Nowadays, we break the ice to keep a conversation flowing!

Bright-eyed and bushy-tailed

Meaning to be alert and be ready for action.

Examples After a two-hour nap, the baby woke up bright-eyed and bushy-tailed.

Could someone please tell that bright-eyed and bushy-tailed young man to stop making such a racket?

Origin The reference here is to a squirrel. This animal is always alert, and constantly on the move. It is ready for action.

Bring home the bacon

Meaning to provide food for the family; to be a bread-winner.

Examples Bhaskar is married, but it's his wife who brings home the bacon.

Prakash's parents have been telling him to get a job so that he can bring home the bacon.

Origin Bacon is the salted or smoked meat that comes from the back or sides of a pig. In the old days, weekly and monthly fairs were very common in villages. On these occasions, farmers used to bring vegetables, meat, cattle, sheep, etc. and sell them at the market place. As a form of entertainment, a well-greased pig was let loose in the market. Any man or woman who caught the pig could claim it as his/her prize. The person who managed to perform this rather difficult task was literally bringing home the bacon!

Brown noser

Meaning a sycophant; someone who flatters another individual for personal gain.

Examples The brown noser, Vikram, gave his boss a bottle of wine on his birthday.

When did Desai become such a brown noser?

Origin In order to please others, these individuals stoop so low that they often end up rubbing their nose in the dirt, and in the process get it (their nose) brown!

Bull in a china shop

Meaning — a clumsy person who keeps breaking things accidentally. It can also be used to refer to a thoughtless or tactless person.

Examples — Please don't let Aruna come into this room. She's like a bull in a china shop.

Govinda is very rude, a real bull in a china shop.

Origin — If you were to let a bull loose in a shop filled with delicate china, what do you think will happen to the crockery? Chances are the animal will end up breaking everything. A bull is mostly known for its brute strength.

Bum's rush

Meaning — to get rid of a person as quickly as possible, often using force. In most cases, you grab hold of the person and throw him out. It is also possible to say, 'get the bum's rush'; the expression is American in origin.

Examples — I think Sangeeta and Sajida are up to something. I got the bum's rush when I walked into their apartment.

When the well-known artist walked into the club wearing slippers, he was given the bum's rush by the two security guards.

Origin The 'bum' in the expression refers to a homeless person who begs for a living. When such a person enters a shop or a hotel, how do owners respond? They promptly catch hold of him, and rush him out the door. Hence the expression, 'the bum's rush'.

Burn one's boats

Meaning to commit oneself to a course of action; to cut off all escape routes.

Examples Be careful about what you are going to say. You may end up burning your boats.

Mithun knew that by supporting his boss, he was burning his boats.

Origin In the old days, it was common practice among military commanders to burn their boats or ships when they landed on foreign soil. They did this to prevent soldiers from running away if things did not go according to plan. By burning the boats, the commander ensured that the only way the soldiers were going back home was by defeating the enemy. The idiom has the same meaning as 'burn one's bridges'.

Burn the candle at both ends

Meaning to exhaust or make too great a demand on one's energy.

Examples Ram had a night job and a day job. He was burning the candle at both ends.

After burning the candle at both ends for several weeks, Radhika fell ill.

Origin A candle that is lit at both ends burns out very quickly.

Burn the midnight oil

Meaning to work late into the night.

Examples Our students start burning the midnight oil a week before the exams.

Prema said she would be burning the midnight oil tonight.

Origin The expression came into being much before electricity was discovered. In the old days, when scholars wished to read or study late into the night, they made use of oil lamps. So, when a person said he was burning the midnight oil, he meant he was working by the light of a lamp.

Bury the hatchet

Meaning making peace with an individual by resolving your differences with him/her.

Examples After twenty years of being at war, the two countries decided to bury the hatchet.

It's about time the two of you buried the hatchet.

Origin A 'hatchet' is an axe. Burying the hatchet was something that the Native Americans used to do when they wanted to make peace with someone. Unfortunately for them, they performed a similar ritual with the white men who had settled in New England. In 1680, Samuel Sewell wrote: "Meeting with the Sachem (Indian chiefs), they came to an agreement and buried two axes in the ground, which ceremony to them is more significant and binding than all the Articles of Peace, the hatchet being the principal weapon." The white man did not think much of this ritual because years later he slaughtered Native Americans by the thousands, and herded those who were alive into what are now called 'reservations'.

Bury your head in the sand

Meaning to deliberately ignore or turn a blind eye to danger or a problem in the hope that it will somehow go away on its own.

Examples You cannot continue to bury your head in the sand. We have a serious problem on hand.

Opposition members said that corruption was being ignored, and accused the PM of burying his head in the sand.

Origin When an ostrich is in danger, it lies flat on the ground and stretches out its long neck in order to remain undetected. Many people thought the bird was trying to bury its head in the sand in order to avoid seeing the coming danger. What most people do not realise is that animals are much smarter than human beings!

Busman's holiday

Meaning to spend one's holiday doing what one normally does on any working day.

Examples Raju made his wife cook during the trip. It turned out to be a real busman's holiday for her.

I thought I would make it a busman's holiday and finish writing the report.

Origin The expression comes from the time when buses in London were pulled by horses. Every driver was given his own team of horses, and man and animal worked together every day. As it usually happens in such circumstances, a close relationship developed between the driver and his team. Whenever the driver went on leave, a substitute was hired to 'drive' the bus. Very often, the regular driver would sit in his bus all day as a passenger just to make sure that his horses were being treated properly by the substitute. Since the driver ended up doing what he normally did on any working day, such a holiday began to be called 'busman's holiday'.

Buttonhole someone

Meaning to grab hold of someone and force them to listen to you.

Examples The people buttonholed the candidate and explained their problems.

After the meeting, my friend buttonholed me and asked me about the test.

On the tenth day of our trip, we went to see......

Origin The original expression was 'to button hold someone'. The person forced you to listen to him by holding on to your shirt/coat button. As the years went by, 'button hold' became 'buttonhole'.

(in) Cahoots with

Meaning to conspire with another person; to scheme or plot with someone to get something. The expression has a negative connotation.

Examples Manjit tells me that the Principal is in cahoots with the dealer who supplies the school with computers.

It's common knowledge that our Ministers are in cahoots with organised crime.

Etymology Some believe it comes from the French 'cohorte', meaning 'accomplice'.

Pronunciation The 'a' in the first syllable is pronounced like the 'a' in 'china', and the 'oo' is like the 'oo' in 'pool' and 'cool'. The word is pronounced 'ke-**HOOTS**', with the stress on the second syllable.

Cakewalk

Meaning something very easily achieved; completing a task without having to put in too much of an effort.

Examples Given your experience, getting the job should be a cakewalk.

The first couple of rounds of the tournament should be a cakewalk.

Origin The 'cakewalk' was a form of entertainment among African Americans. Well-dressed couples who took part in this competition were made to walk around a cake. The pair that performed this task most gracefully was awarded a prize. In most cases, the prize was the cake itself; the winner used to 'take the cake'. Later, the word 'cakewalk' was used to refer to a popular form of dance.

Call a spade a spade

Meaning to speak in a straightforward, blunt manner.

Examples I don't think Ravi is the sort of person who would call a spade a spade.

I like talking to villagers. They call a spade a spade.

Origin The idiom is a translation of an old Greek proverb, 'to call a fig a fig and a spade a spade.' The expression was translated into Latin, and was later introduced into English by John Knox, a Protestant reformer. The 'spade' has nothing to do with the game of cards; it refers to the implement used in the garden.

Call the shots

Meaning someone who decides what must be done; this individual is in total control of the situation. The expression is limited to informal contexts.

Examples It is not the Vice Chancellor, but the students who are calling the shots.

Why do you blame me? I wasn't the person calling the shots.

Origin According to some scholars, the expression comes from the world of target shooting. A good marksman, before firing his gun, usually informs his audience which target he will be hitting. He also tells them the exact location on the target he is aiming for. Others believe that the expression comes from the game of billiards. In this game, a player announces in advance which ball he is going to be hitting next, and which pocket it will fall into.

Called on the carpet

Meaning to be questioned by someone in authority; to be rebuked and held accountable for a mistake or an offense.

Examples The students were called on the carpet for cheating in the exam.

The new employee was called on the carpet for taking too many tea breaks.

Origin In the old days, most offices did not have a carpet. Only the most important people in the organisation were given one. Therefore, when you say that someone was called on the carpet, what you mean is that a person in a subordinate position was called to the boss' room to face the music. The person literally stood on the carpet while the boss gave him a piece of his mind.

Can't hold a candle to someone

Meaning not be equal to someone.

Examples As a teacher, Satish cannot hold a candle to Atul.

According to Manaswini, no pop group can hold a candle to *The Beatles*.

Origin The expression has been around for several hundred years. In the old days, when street lighting was almost non-existent, the fairly well-to-do people had servants who followed them everywhere with a candle; those who did not have servants, hired 'linkboys'. These boys carried lanterns and candles, and they provided the necessary light for people to get from one part of the town to another. Since the servants and the linkboys werc looked down upon by the masters, the expression 'can't hold a candle to someone' began to mean, 'someone who is inferior'.

Can't see the wood for the trees

Meaning missing the big picture by focusing on the non-essential things. It is also possible to say 'can't see the forest for the trees'.

Examples From the questions that were asked after the presentation, it was fairly obvious that most of the participants couldn't see the wood for the trees.

Brilliant as he was, Dravid sometimes couldn't see the forest for the trees.

Origin Sometimes, we focus our attention on the beauty of a single tree, instead of taking in the grandeur or magnificence of the forest.

Canary in a coal mine

Meaning someone or something that serves as a warning to others; the person or thing is an indicator that the situation is becoming dangerous. The expression is not heard very frequently nowadays.

Examples Before entering the tunnel, we sent in the convicts to see if the air was poisonous. They were merely canaries in a coal mine.

According to this article, the melting of glaciers in the Arctic is a canary in the coal mine for global warming.

Origin For many centuries, miners used to carry a caged canary with them when they went to work. These small songbirds were used to determine how good or bad the air was inside the mines. Since mines in the past did not always have a good ventilation system, deadly gases like methane and carbon monoxide would often build up in the shafts, making them dangerous places for people to work in. The canary was very sensitive to these odourless gases; even a small amount was enough to kill the bird. As long as the bird kept chirping, the miners knew that the air was safe; but if the bird curled up and died, it served as a warning to the people that they must leave the place immediately.

Carrot and stick approach

Meaning to reward those who do their job, and punish those who do not.

Examples The Government says it favours a carrot and stick approach to get the unemployed people back to work.

Teachers use both the carrot and the stick to make sure students do their work.

Origin The carrot and stick approach was first used by owners of donkeys in order to keep their animals moving. Whenever the animal stopped, the rider used to dangle a raw carrot in front of the animal's nose. If the stubborn animal still refused to move, the owner gave it a sound thrashing with a stick!

Carry coals to Newcastle

Meaning to do something unnecessary. It is also possible to say, 'take coals to Newcastle'.

Examples Mohan was trying to sell ice cream to the Italians. That's like carrying coals to Newcastle.

Exporting pine to Scandinavia is like carrying coals to Newcastle.

Origin Newcastle is a place in the north of England, and it is famous for its coal mines! So if you are carrying coals to Newcastle, you are merely wasting your energy.

Catch a few rays

Meaning to lie down or sit outside in the sun.

Examples Kapil spent the early morning on the beach, catching some rays.

I think I'll read the paper outside and catch a few rays.

Origin The 'rays' in this informal expression refers to the rays of the sun.

Catch as catch can

Meaning resorting to any method available to complete a task without being unduly worried about the ethics. Perform tasks in an unplanned and unsystematic manner.

Examples When his former partner complained that he was taking away his clients, Rahul told him that in business it was a case of catch as catch can.

The crew was intent on finishing the project in record time. As a result, sleeping and eating were catch as catch can.

Origin Are you a fan of WWF wrestling? If you are, then you will understand what the word 'catch' refers to. In freestyle wrestling, there are no restrictions on how you can hold your opponent. You can 'catch' or hold him/her in any way you want. The idiom has more or less the same meaning as 'no holds barred'.

Catch-22

Meaning a no-win situation. No matter what you do, you end up on the losing side.

Example The companies didn't want to hire Velu because he didn't have any work experience. But he wasn't going to get any experience unless someone hired him. It was a real Catch-22 situation.

Origin The expression comes from the title of a novel written by Joseph Heller in 1961. Many people consider this work of fiction, set during the Second World War, a classic. In the novel, the only way that pilots could get out of combat duty was by pleading insanity. In order to be discharged, these individuals had to claim they were insane. But the catch was that only a sane person would know that going on bombing missions was dangerous. Therefore, when a pilot pleaded insanity, he was doing what any sane person would! Asking to be certified was the act of a perfectly sane man! Result? No discharge.

Cat's whiskers

Meaning to think you are better than others; the best in the group.

Examples Cinderella probably thought she was the cat's whiskers in her new dress.

Many of our film stars think they are the cat's whiskers.

Origin Some people believe that the expression was coined by the American cartoonist, Thomas A.

Dorgan. Others believe that the term refers to the fine adjustable wire used in a crystal radio.

Caught in the crossfire

Meaning getting caught in the middle of a fight.

Examples My uncle and aunt were having an argument, and unfortunately Das got caught in the crossfire.

When my sister and her friend have an argument, they try to draw me into it. But I always make sure that I don't get caught in the crossfire.

Origin When two people are shooting at each other, you should not stand in the line of fire.

Chalk and cheese

Meaning two things that are very different from each other; they have nothing in common. The expression has been part of the English language for a very long time. It is also possible to say 'as different as chalk from cheese'. The expression has the same meaning as 'apples and oranges'.

Examples I can't believe that Suresh and Vijay are brothers. They're like chalk and cheese.

I don't understand why they call them 'Twin Cities'. They are as different as chalk from cheese.

Origin According to some scholars, John Gower was the first person to use the idiom in his text, *Confessio Amantis*, written in 1390.

Chasing rainbows

Meaning trying to achieve something that is impossible; trying to do something which you are not really capable of.

Examples Raju says he wants to be the next Federer. I think he is chasing rainbows.

My cousin wanted to go into business, but his parents and close friends told him to quit chasing rainbows.

Origin Chasing a rainbow is a meaningless activity. It is a total waste of time because you will never succeed in catching one.

Cheek by jowl

Meaning very close together, side by side.

Examples The students had to walk cheek by jowl along the narrow corridors.

In some cities, several families live cheek by jowl in a single house.

Origin In the case of some people, the loose flesh in their lower cheeks hangs towards their jaw. This bit of loose flesh is called 'jowl'. Since the cheek is very close to the jowl, the expression 'cheek by jowl' means 'very close together'.

Pronunciation 'Jowl' rhymes with 'owl', 'howl' and 'growl'.

Chew the fat

Meaning have an informal chat with someone; complain or argue about something.

Examples The students chewed the fat for some time, and decided not to lodge a complaint against the Registrar.

Nothing much happened. We chewed the fat for half an hour and left.

Origin In the old days, when the food supply began to run low on a ship, sailors were given salted pork and beef to chew on. It was very difficult to chew the tough meat, and sailors often grumbled or complained about the quality of food. It is also possible to say, 'chew the rag'.

Chickens have come home to roost

Meaning to face the consequences of the deeds done in the past. If you do something bad, it will come back to bite or haunt you.

Examples Ganesh is going out of his way to hurt people's feelings. He doesn't realise that the chickens will come home to roost someday.

The Minister was sent to prison 30 years after committing the crime. The chickens finally came home to roost, I guess.

Origin The original form of this 700-year-old expression was 'curses are like chickens; they always come home to roost'. The bad deeds that one may commit in one's lifetime are compared with chickens. Hens and chickens in farms usually potter around all day looking for food. When the sun is about to set, they return to the safety of their henhouse to roost. When used as a noun, the word 'roost' refers to the place where birds rest. It could be anywhere – the branch of a tree, a henhouse, etc. When a bird roosts somewhere, it rests there. Geoffrey Chaucer is believed to have used this expression in his *Canterbury Tales*.

Chink in the armour

Meaning a flaw which can be taken advantage of by other people. The expression can be used with things as well.

Examples The up-and-coming star spent hours looking for a chink in the champion's armour.

If you ask me, Revathi's fiery temper is the only chink in her armour.

Origin 'Chink' is a rather obscure word meaning 'slit' or 'narrow opening'. In the old days, as a form of protection, soldiers used to wear armour. If the armour had a slit, then it became a weak spot, which enemies took advantage of.

Chip off the old block

Meaning a son who behaves or looks like his father.

Examples Bala is definitely a chip off the old block.

Damodaran is a chip off the old block. He's a teacher, just like his father.

Origin The 'block' here refers to a block of wood, and the 'chip' is a small piece which has been broken off the block of wood. The characteristics of the chip will be similar to those of the wood.

Chip on one's shoulder

Meaning to have an attitude problem; itching for a fight.

Examples Ever since Rahul's promotion, Harish has had a chip on his shoulder.

I'd be careful with Udaya. She has a chip on her shoulder.

Origin The expression is American in origin. In the past, children who were angry about something and were itching for a fight would walk around with a piece of wood (chip) on their shoulder. This was a challenge to others, daring them to knock the chip off the shoulder. When someone did, it always resulted in a fight.

Chips are down

Meaning to be in a difficult or dangerous situation.

Examples When the chips were down, all the employees rallied around the Chairman.

Tiwari was always there to help out when the chips were down.

Origin The 'chips' referred to here are not potato chips, but the ones generally used in gambling. In movies, when the hero and the villain play cards, they keep increasing the stakes by throwing plastic chips on the table. These coloured chips are a substitute for money. So when you are gambling and you find that your chips are down, it means you are losing. You are in a 'difficult situation' because there is hardly any money left.

Chomp at the bit

Meaning to become impatient; to be anxious to do something. It is possible to say 'champ at the bit' as well.

Examples The players were chomping at the bit to enter the field.

The lecture was so boring that all the students were chomping at the bit to leave.

Origin The expression comes from the world of horses. The 'bit' refers to a horse's mouthpiece – the metal piece that a rider puts in the mouth of the animal in order to direct and control it. When you 'chomp' or 'champ' on something, you chew or munch on it rather noisily. When a horse gets restless or impatient, it begins to 'chomp' on the 'bit'.

Clarion call

Meaning an urgent call for immediate action.

Examples The Minister issued a clarion call to the students to join the protest.

The results of the studies are a clarion call to the President to take climate change seriously.

Origin A 'clarion' is a trumpet with a narrow tube which makes a very shrill sound when blown. The word comes from the Latin 'clarus', meaning 'clear'. The high-pitched trumpet was mostly used in the past to alert soldiers during battles.

Pronunciation The 'a' sounds like the 'a' in 'cat', 'bat' and 'hat'. The word is pronounced '**KLA**-ri-en'.

Clean bill of health

Meaning an object or a person that is in good condition/ health.

Examples The doctors carried out several tests before giving Radha a clean bill of health.

Of the twenty buildings inspected, only four were given a clean bill of health.

Origin In the old days, the captain of a ship was handed over a document by the port authority which certified that there was no infection or epidemic at the port from which the vessel set sail. This document was called the Bill of Health, and unless it was presented at the next port, the ship was refused entry.

Cleanse the Augean stables

Meaning an expression mostly used in politics to mean, 'to clean up a mess' in a very short period of time; to root out corruption. It has the same meaning as 'to clean house'.

Examples Talking about corruption, the Prime Minster said that he would cleanse the Augean stables in a hundred days.

Gayathri has been sent to cleanse the Augean stables of the previous administration.

Origin King Augeas of Elis had huge stables containing about 3000 oxen. According to legend, these stables were extremely dirty because they had not been cleaned in thirty years. Hercules was given twelve tasks by Zeus, and was told that if he completed all of them successfully, he would become immortal. One of the 'labours' he was given was to 'cleanse the Augean stables' in a single day. Hercules completed this task successfully by diverting the course of the river Alpheus, and letting the water run through the huge stables.

Pronunciation The 'au' in the first syllable is like the 'ore' in 'shore', 'chore' and 'pore'. The 'g' is like the 'j' in 'jam', 'jail' and 'job'. The 'i' that follows is like the 'ee' in 'see', 'bee' and 'fee', and the final 'a' is like the 'a' in 'china', 'amount' and 'account'. The word is pronounced 'au-**JEE**-en', with the stress on the second syllable.

Closed book

Meaning not to know anything about something; a mystery.

Examples The serial killer's early life is a closed book.

Mars is no longer a closed book for scientists.

Origin A book that remains closed can never be read. If it is never read, the contents always remain a mystery.

Cloud-cuckoo-land

Meaning a place where everything is perfect; being unrealistically idealistic, naive.

Examples If you think Sarita is going to return the money, you're living in cloud-cuckoo-land.

Devi thinks that even without any experience, she can find a job that will pay her ₹70,000 a month. I told her she was living in cloud-cuckoo-land.

Origin The expression comes from *The Birds*, a play written by Aristophanes, an Athenian playwright. In the play, the characters grow tired of the imperfections on earth, and decide to build the perfect city among the clouds. They call this place 'Cloud Cuckoo Land'.

(on) Cloud nine

Meaning feeling extremely happy; feeling on top of the world.

Examples When the results were announced, Neena was on cloud nine for several weeks.

The entire team was on cloud nine after winning the championship.

Origin No one is really sure where the expression comes from. Some believe that the original expression was 'on cloud seven', very similar to the expression 'seventh heaven'. Others believe that nine was chosen because it is considered a mystical number. According to weathermen, 'cloud nine' refers to the 'cumulonimbus' or the thunderstorm cloud. This cloud often rises to 40,000 feet; and when you are 'on' such a cloud, you are literally on top of the world! The expression was made popular in the 1950s by a radio series titled *Johnny Dollar*. In the series, the hero is often knocked unconscious; when he is in this state, he is transported to cloud nine, from where he continues to talk to his listeners.

(in) Clover

Meaning: to be content; to live in comfort and have no financial worries.

Examples: They struggled for over twenty years, and now they're in clover.

After we sell the rights to this movie, we'll be in clover.

Origin: Clover is a plant which is used as food for livestock – animals usually found on farms. If an animal were allowed to eat as much clover as it wanted to, how would it feel? Pretty happy, don't you think?

Cock a snook at

Meaning to show defiance; express scorn at someone in authority.

Examples Roshni cocked a snook at the policeman, and kept on driving.

Sajit cocked a snook at the teacher, tore up the report card and walked out.

Origin The word 'snook' means 'nose'. When you cock a snook at someone, you place your thumb on the tip of your nose, and point the remaining four fingers at the person you are making fun of, and wiggle them. This is something that children do when they wish to ridicule someone.

Cock-and-bull story

Meaning a lie; a story that cannot be believed.

Examples When I asked Namratha why she hadn't done her assignment, she gave me some cock-and-bull story about having been abducted by aliens.

When the Chairman asked for an explanation, all he got from the Vice President was some cock-and-bull story.

Origin Some scholars believe that the idiom has its origins in the fables that we all read as children;

stories in which animals behave and talk like human beings. Such stories are often considered to be unrealistic by people who are very practical in their outlook. They cannot imagine that animals like lions, bulls, foxes, etc. can actually talk. Some others believe that 'Cock' and 'Bull' refer to two taverns. People who went to these bars got drunk and told tall tales.

Cold feet

Meaning — to lose courage, and end up losing one's confidence.

Examples — Ganesh and Jyothi were planning to get married next month. But Ganesh got cold feet and called off the wedding.

Avinash agreed to sing at the local club. But he developed cold feet and cancelled the event.

Origin — It comes from the Italian expression 'avegh minga frecc i pee', which literally means 'to have cold feet'. The expression, however, was mainly used to mean 'to be without money'. It was in this sense that the 16th century dramatist, Ben Jonson, used it in his play, *Volpone*. It was in the 1890s in America that the expression acquired the meaning 'cowardice'.

Cold storage

Meaning: to put aside temporarily; to put something on the backburner.

Examples: Ratan's plans of buying a house were put in cold storage when he lost his job.

It's a brilliant idea. But given the current situation, we'll have to keep it in cold storage.

Origin: A cold storage is a place where perishables are stored. Once something is put in this room, you can forget about it because the cold temperature will ensure that it stays fresh.

Cook someone's goose

Meaning: to spoil someone's chances or plans; to ruin someone.

Examples: Amitabh's goose was cooked when they found the stolen idol in his safe.

If you continue to treat Neethu the way you do, she'll cook your goose.

Origin: According to some sources, when King Eric, the mad king of Sweden, tried to capture a small town, the locals ridiculed his army by hanging a goose to shoot at. This insult made Eric so angry that he not only burnt the town down, but also cooked the goose and ate it!

Cost an arm and a leg

Meaning: pay very dearly for something; pay a lot of money for something.

Examples: The tickets for the one-day match cost Manju an arm and a leg.

I am not going to pay an arm and a leg for a piece of junk like that.

Origin: The arm and the leg are important parts of the body. There are many actions that one will be unable to perform if they are missing. Other expressions which have the same meaning are 'pay an arm and a leg' and 'pay through one's nose'.

Cross the bridge when you come to it

Meaning: do not worry about things that may or may not happen in the future.

Examples: What if we run out of funding? We'll cross the bridge when we come to it.

Mohan seemed unconcerned. He said that he would cross the bridge when he came to it.

Origin: It is self explanatory.

Cross the Rubicon

Meaning: to commit oneself to a course of action from which there is no going back; to reach a point of no return.

Examples: Rajeev knew that he would be crossing the Rubicon by testifying against his boss.

By giving a handsome down payment on the house, Ananth had crossed the Rubicon.

Origin: Rubicon is the name of a river. In Roman times, it served as a boundary between Italy and France. Julius Caesar crossed it in 49 BC to wage war against Rome.

Curate's egg

Meaning: something that is partly good and partly bad.

Examples: My favourite hero's latest film is a bit of a curate's egg.

The University is something of a curate's egg – elegant old buildings surrounded by ugly modern architecture.

Origin: The expression became quite popular because of a cartoon drawn by George du Maurier in *Punch* magazine in 1895. The cartoon shows a curate and a bishop eating breakfast. The curate, unfortunately, has been served a bad egg. The bishop remarks, "I am afraid you have got a bad egg." Since the curate doesn't want to offend his host, he replies, "Oh no, My Lord, I assure you! Parts of it are excellent!"

Pronunciation The 'u' is like the 'ure' in 'pure', 'sure' and 'cure' and the 'a' sounds like the 'a' in 'china'. One way of pronouncing the word is '**KYUE-ret**' with the stress on the first syllable.

Curl one's hair

Meaning to shock, frighten or alarm someone.

Examples I thought the new horror movie would make my hair curl. I was disappointed.

The speed at which Harish drove was enough to curl my hair.

Origin The idiom is not meant to be taken literally. When a person is really frightened by something, his hair does not curl, but stands up.

Curry favour

Meaning try to gain a person's approval by flattering him/her; attempt to win a person's support by talking to him rather politely, very often resorting to insincere praise. The expression is normally used to show disapproval.

Examples Prakash is trying to curry favour with his uncle again.

If I were you, I wouldn't attempt to curry favour with anyone.

Origin The 'curry' in the expression has nothing to do with the curry we eat. This curry comes from the world of horse riding. People who take care of horses make use of a 'curry-comb' to rub the animal down. It is from this that we get the expression 'to curry', meaning 'to groom or rub down a horse'. The word 'favour' in the idiom is a corruption of the French name 'Favel' (also spelt 'Fauvel'). Favel is the name of a cunning centaur that appears in a French story written in the 14th century. A 'centaur', as you probably know, is an animal that is half man and half horse. In the story, people who wanted to be in the good books of the evil Favel used to flatter him and also rub him down. In other words, the characters in the story used to 'curry Favel'. In fact, the original expression was 'to curry Favel'. Since 'Favel' sounded like 'favour', native speakers of English started saying, 'to curry favour'.

Cut a caper

Meaning to leap or dance about in a playful manner. Nowadays, the expression is mainly used to mean 'a lively or playful leap'. The expression can also be used to mean 'to play a trick on someone'.

Examples When he heard that he had been promoted, Bala cut a little caper before walking into the boss' room.

The bowler cut a caper when he got his fifth wicket.

Origin A 'caper' is a lively skip or hop. Shakespeare coined this expression in *Twelfth Night*.

Pronunciation The word 'caper' rhymes with 'paper'.

Cut and dried

Meaning a decision that is final, something that cannot be changed; uninteresting.

Examples Shalini's plans are cut and dried. You cannot make any changes now.

Hemant's talk was cut and dried. He must brush up on his presentation skills.

Origin According to some scholars, the cut and dried material refers to timber. Wood that has been dried after cutting is ready for use. One can use it to light a fire. Some others believe that the idiom refers to the cut and dried herbs available in shops, which can be readily used in one's cooking.

Cut and run

Meaning to run away from one's problems.

Examples When the pressure began to mount, many in the Management decided to cut and run.

Raju's cowardly decision to cut and run was criticised by everyone.

Origin The expression comes from the world of sailing. In the old days, when a ship that was at anchor came under attack, the sailors, in order to make a quick getaway, cut the rope to which the anchor was tied. Instead of going through the lengthy process of raising the anchor and then setting sail, they merely 'cut' the rope and allowed the ship to 'run' before the wind.

Cut loose

Meaning to free oneself from something or someone; to act without restraint.

Examples When Prahlad, Bala and Rakesh get together, they really cut loose.

I've never seen Meera behave that way. She really cut loose after lunch.

Origin Removing the rope that an animal has been tied to for a long time.

Cut no ice

Meaning to have no effect on someone; not to be influenced or impressed by something.

Examples The excuses I gave cut no ice with the new teacher.

The romantic sob story cut no ice with the audience.

Origin In the old days, when the river/sea froze, sailors used to get off the ship to break the ice that was blocking their passage. Ice is a very hard substance, and it requires an extraordinarily strong instrument to break it. Ordinary tools will make no impression on it: they will not cut the ice.

Cut off one's nose to spite one's face

Meaning to harm oneself much more than the person one is trying to hurt.

Examples Harish loves to play tennis, but he refused to play because he doesn't like Suresh. He was cutting off his nose to spite his face.

Daya cut off her nose to spite her face when she refused to come to the industrial exhibition with us.

Origin The expression has been around for quite some time. If you wanted to get even with someone, or hurt the feelings of that person, would you do it by cutting off your nose? Probably not! It wouldn't be a very sensible thing to do. The expression first appeared in print in the late 18th century, and some believe that it is a translation of the French 'Se couper le nez pour faire depit a son visage.'

Cut to the quick/bone

Meaning someone's comments that hurt an individual very badly. Something that the individual said causes you a great deal of distress; the comments wound you emotionally. It is also possible to say 'cut someone to the bone'.

Examples The comments that Janani made at the meeting cut me to the quick/bone.

The things that Krishna accused me of cut me to the quick.

Origin The expression is seldom heard nowadays as it is considered rather old fashioned. 'Quick' comes from the Old English 'ciwicu', meaning 'living'. In the context of the idiom, the word refers to the sensitive skin under one's fingernails and toenails. When we cut our nails to the quick, we cut them very short, and this often results in some amount of bleeding and a lot of pain. The literal meaning of this expression is 'to remove or slice the flesh right down to the bone'.

Cut your eye teeth on something

Meaning — to have a lot of experience under your belt; to know all there is to know about something.

Examples — Does Ajay know anything about cars? He cut his eye teeth on them!

If you want to know something about computers, ask Akshay. He cut his eye teeth on them.

Origin — An 'eye tooth' refers to the canine in the upper jaw; the two canines play a very important role when we have to bite into something. The canine is referred to as 'eye tooth' because each is positioned right below the eye.

D-day

Meaning — the day chosen for the commencement of an important activity.

Examples — The players are preparing themselves for D-day.

Remember, next Friday is D-day. We are launching our new product.

Origin — The 'D' in D-day stands for 'day'. So when you say 'D-day', what you are actually saying is 'Day-day'. The expression was first used during the First World War, and not, as many people think, in the Second World War. The famous D-day was 6 June, 1944.

Damp squib

Meaning fail to meet one's expectations; a sense of disappointment.

Examples The seminar was a damp squib because none of the big names turned up.

For the majority of Indians, the World Cup turned out to be a damp squib.

Origin We all know what 'damp' means – it means 'wet'. A 'squib' is a firecracker. We know from experience that when a firecracker that is damp is lit, it will fail to explode. How do we feel when this happens? Terribly disappointed!

Dark horse

Meaning a person whose ability one knows very little about. Someone whose abilities, plans and feelings are a mystery to others.

Examples According to my favourite columnist, there are two or three dark horses in the tournament.

I didn't know that Vinita could paint. She's such a dark horse.

Origin The expression comes from the world of horse racing. In order to determine the odds on a horse winning a race, punters take into account the animal's lineage and its win–loss record. If this information is not available, then those placing bets have no way of knowing the strengths and weaknesses of the animal. They are in the 'dark' about the animal. Such a horse is a 'dark horse'. It is believed that Benjamin Disraeli was the first person to use this expression.

Davy Jones's locker

Meaning to drown; to go to the bottom of the sea.

Examples The old pirate ended up in Davy Jones's locker.

According to this newspaper report, the treasure is still in Davy Jones's locker.

Origin Although the idiom has been a part of the English language for well over two centuries, no one is really sure about its origin. Some scholars speculate that Davy Jones or David Jones was a fearsome pirate. One of the things that he did with his prisoners was to make them walk the plank. In other words, he threw them overboard while they were in the middle of the ocean. Result? The prisoners invariably drowned. Another theory is that David Jones was the owner of a pub who often drugged his unsuspecting patrons and sold them off as slaves to ship owners. The theory that most people are comfortable with is the following. Jones is actually from Jonah, and Davy is a corruption of the West Indian word 'duppy', meaning 'ghost' or 'devil'. So Davy Jones is actually the spirit of the sea, the sailor's devil!

Dead in the water

Meaning a failure; no matter what you do, things will not improve. Frequently used in American English in informal contexts.

Examples With the sudden increase in interest rates, our plans for expansion are dead in the water, I'm afraid.

The economy of the country has been dead in the water for some years.

Origin According to some scholars, the 'dead' object in the water refers to a ship. In the past, a ship that remained stationary or immobile because of insufficient wind was said to be 'dead'. Like any dead individual, the ship showed no signs of life – no movement. Others believe that the dead object in the water is a fish.

Deep pockets

Meaning a very wealthy person; an organisation with a lot of money.

Examples In our country, the Ambanis and the Tatas have deep pockets.

If the school is keen on improving the facilities, then the Management must find some deep pockets to finance the project.

Origin — If your pockets are 'deep', that is, they go a long way down, then it becomes possible for you to stuff a lot of money into them.

Devil's advocate

Meaning — to pretend to be against something that someone has said; to say something in order to make the other person consider his argument in greater detail. To compel an individual to examine the merits and demerits of his case.

Examples — Are those your actual beliefs or are you merely playing the devil's advocate?

Praneetha was playing the devil's advocate just to provoke the two of you.

Origin — The term is a translation of the Latin 'Advocatus Diaboli'; it was first used by the authorities in Church. Whenever people demanded that someone be made a saint (canonised), the Roman Catholic Church appointed a devil's advocate. It was the job of this official to argue why the individual should not be made a saint.

Ding-dong battle

Meaning — to be involved in a long-drawn-out battle; the fight is so intense and even that it is very difficult to predict who will emerge the winner. It has the same meaning as 'see-saw battle'.

Examples — The fans were hoping for a ding-dong battle. They were disappointed when the Aussies thrashed the Indians.

The fight between the Union and the Management is turning out to be a ding-dong battle.

Origin — The 'ding-dong' refers to the sound that a bell makes; the back and forth motion of the knocker hitting a bell.

Dog days

Meaning — the hottest days of summer.

Examples — During the dog days of summer, we get water every other day.

The heat is unbearable. How are we going to cope with the dog days?

Origin — The hottest days in Europe mostly occur in the month of July. According to an old superstition, this was also the period when dogs had a tendency to go mad. But contrary to popular belief, 'dog days' has nothing to do with dogs on earth; it has more to do with the dog in the sky! In this case, it refers to Sirius, the Dog Star. In the height of summer, the Dog Star rises along with the sun. The ancient Romans believed that this star added to the heat of the sun, and in the process caused the weather to become unbearably hot. The expression 'dog days' is a translation of the Latin, 'caniculares dies'.

Dog in the manger

Meaning — a spoilsport; someone who has something that he does not need or make use of, but is unwilling to give it to a person who might have use for it.

Examples — Stop being such a dog in the manger, Jyotsna. If you're not going to be using that racquet, let me have it.

Aditya's dog-in-the-manger attitude is unlikely to win him friends.

Origin — A manger is an open box or container filled with grass or hay from which cows and horses feed. The expression 'dog in the manger' comes from a story in *Aesop's Fables*, in which a dog sitting in a manger drives away the cows which come to eat. Although the surly dog has no use for the hay, it is not willing to let the cows enjoy their food.

Pronunciation 'Manger' rhymes with 'danger', 'ranger' and 'stranger'.

Dog's breakfast

Meaning — to make a complete mess of something.

Examples — Deepa made a bit of a dog's breakfast of the essay.

Jai made a real dog's breakfast of painting the kitchen.

Origin — Dogs have the habit of getting up early and going out. And when they do go out, they eat anything they find on the road. This informal expression is mostly limited to British English.

Dog-eared

Meaning — to fold the top corner of a page in a book in order to remember which page to return to; a page folded in this manner is said to be 'dog-eared'. The expression can also be used to mean 'shabby from overuse'.

Examples — The old trunk in the garage contained many of my sister's dog-eared notebooks.

You normally find dog-eared magazines in our library.

Origin — The ears of dogs very often flop over.

Done and dusted

Meaning: to complete something successfully; limited to informal contexts.

Examples: Saif wants the project to be done and dusted by tomorrow.

The match had been done and dusted by the end of the third day.

Origin: In the past, everyone made use of ink to write; people dipped their quill or pen into a bottle of ink before putting words on paper. Sometimes, they had to wait for a long time for the paper to absorb the ink. To quicken the drying process, people sprinkled an absorbent dust or powder on the paper. Once the ink had dried, the powder was dusted off the paper.

Donkey's years

Meaning: a very long time. It is also possible to say 'donkey's ages'.

Examples: It's been donkey's years since I spoke to Sarita and Ganesh.

The project has been going on for donkey's ages.

Origin: The expression has nothing to do with the lifespan of a donkey. It has more to do with the animal's

Meet our Finance Officer. As you can see, he has been with us for donkey's years.

enormously long ears! The original expression was 'donkey's ears', and not 'years'.

Don't count your chickens before they hatch

Meaning warning someone not to celebrate prematurely.

Examples Ask Suresh. He may be willing to lend you some money. But don't count your chickens before they hatch.

Stop talking about the places you are going to see. You haven't got your visa as yet. Don't count your chickens before they hatch.

Origin The expression comes from a story in *Aesop's Fables*. In the story, a woman is carrying a basket of eggs. While she is walking, she begins to think about how many chicks she will soon have, how much money she will make by selling the chicks, the things she will buy with all the money, etc. As she is thinking about all this, she drops the basket of eggs! Result? The woman is left with no eggs and no chicks!

Don't look a gift horse in the mouth

Meaning do not find fault with something that has been given to you as a gift.

Examples Mohan complained about the secondhand cycle that his aunt had given him. I told him not to look a gift horse in the mouth.

Anand always complains about the gifts I give him. He shouldn't look a gift horse in the mouth.

Origin The normal way to determine a horse's age and its condition is to look at its teeth. If the teeth are long, it indicates that the animal is old and not in good condition. When you are given a horse as a gift, you are not expected to open its mouth and see if the animal is in good condition.

Dot the i's and cross the t's

Meaning to do a meticulous job; to pay great attention to every detail, even minor ones, and ensure there are no mistakes in something you do.

Examples Before handing over the proposal to the Chairman, Sajida ensured that she had dotted all the i's and crossed all the t's.

Please ask Rajiv to take a look at your dissertation. He'll make sure that the i's have been dotted and the t's crossed.

Origin According to one theory, when children learn how to write, they are told time and again by the teacher to put a dot on top of the letter 'i' and a dash across the letter 't'. If these minor details are overlooked, then the child's writing task is considered incomplete.

Doubting Thomas

Meaning a sceptic; someone who demands proof before he believes or accepts anything.

Examples Balagopal is a real doubting Thomas. He wouldn't believe that the new house was mine till I showed him the documents.

I'm willing to approve the project provided you win over Raju, the doubting Thomas in our department.

Origin When St. Thomas was informed that Christ had risen from the dead, he refused to believe it. He demanded physical proof of Jesus' resurrection. Only when he saw Jesus with his own eyes and touched His wounds did he believe the others. According to scholars, the expression began to be used in the late 19th century. The earlier expressions that were commonly used were 'wavering Thomas' and 'unbelieving Thomas'.

Draw first blood

Meaning to strike the first blow; to hurt the opponent before he hurts you.

Examples In the debate, it was the visitors who drew first blood.

We were hoping to draw first blood; unfortunately, we didn't.

Origin The expression comes from the sport of boxing. In a boxing bout, you attempt to hurt the opponent before he hurts you. You hit him so hard, he starts to bleed.

Dress (up) to the nines

Meaning to be dressed elegantly; wearing one's best clothes.

Examples Mayank was dressed to the nines when he went to meet the Chairman.

Tara makes it a point to dress up to the nines whenever she goes out.

Origin The expression comes from the Middle English, 'dressed up to the eyenes' (eyes). In other words, this is one way of saying that one is immaculately dressed from top to bottom: from the eyes to the feet.

Drink like a fish

Meaning to consume a lot of alcohol.

Examples According to this article, the award-winning writer drinks like a fish.

Our maid told us that her husband drinks like a fish.

Origin A fish, because it always keeps its mouth open, gives the impression that it is constantly drinking water. All it is doing is passing the water through its gills to get the required oxygen to survive.

Drop like a hot potato

Meaning to get rid of something/someone unwanted very quickly.

Examples When Aditya realised she had no money, he dropped her like a hot potato.

The committee dropped the earlier report like a hot potato.

Origin A potato that has been cooked is difficult to handle because it retains heat for a long time. When a potato that is hot is placed in our hand, our immediate reaction is to get rid of it. We drop it quickly.

Drop of a hat

Meaning willing to do something immediately without anyone urging you to.

Examples Kamath was willing to help me with my homework at the drop of a hat.

I would go to Arunachal Pradesh at the drop of a hat.

Origin According to some scholars, the idiom, which comes from the world of boxing, originated in the United States. During the 18th and 19th centuries, bells were not used to inform the fighters when to begin their bout. Instead, a hat or a cap was used. The referee, or the man who was getting the show on the road, raised his hat high and then dropped it. The dropping of the hat signalled to the boxers that they could get on with the fight. Later, the same signalling system began to be used in horse racing. As soon as the man at the starting gate lowered his hat or dropped it, the horses were off and running.

Dry as dust

Meaning something that is dull and boring; not at all engaging.

Examples The speech that the Vice Chancellor gave yesterday was as dry as dust.

The new textbook prescribed for English is as dry as dust.

Origin It is self explanatory.

Dry run

Meaning a rehearsal or practice for a ceremony or procedure. Before the staging of a play, the actors have a dry run – they perform the complete play without stopping.

Examples We made Paul go through a dry run of his presentation.

After several dry runs, Malathy felt confident about being on stage.

Origin According to one theory, the expression comes from the world of firefighting. In the early 18th

century, firemen often demonstrated to the public how they went about putting out fires. If this drill was performed without the use of water, it was called 'dry run'. When water was used, it was called 'wet run'.

Dutch act/cure

Meaning to commit or try to commit suicide.

Examples Many children take the Dutch cure when they fail the Board exam.

The young bride tried the Dutch act when her in-laws began to pester her for more dowry.

Origin The English believed that the average Dutchman was incapable of handling pressure. Instead of facing his problems, he took the easy way out.

Dutch courage

Meaning courage that one displays when one is drunk.

Examples Don't listen to him. That's just Dutch courage talking.

It was Dutch courage that made the Vice Chancellor insult the Minister.

Origin Another idiom which shows the low regard that the English had for the Dutch. They believed that the Dutch were cowards, and the only time they displayed valour was when they were under the influence of alcohol.

Dyed in the wool

Meaning: strong willed, stubborn; someone who has very strong opinions about something; opinions that are not easily changed.

Examples: My cousin Vindya is a dyed-in-the-wool traditionalist. She believes that a woman's place is in the kitchen.

My neighbour claims to be a dyed-in-the-wool communist. But he lives in a huge house and drives a Benz.

Origin: Wool that is dyed before it is spun into yarn retains its colour; the colour becomes permanently fixed.

Ear to the ground

Meaning: being aware of what is happening around you; to be in the know.

Examples: If you want to know what's happening, ask Mani. He has his ear to the ground.

Don't think it is a done deal. Keep your ear to the ground.

Origin: When they went hunting, Native Americans put their ear to the ground in order to detect vibrations of animals moving. By doing this, they could hear the animals long before they saw them.

Earful

Meaning to complain angrily to someone for a long time; to shout at someone. The standard expression is 'give someone an earful'.

Examples The teacher gave the students an earful for not doing their homework.

When I came home late last week, my mother gave me an earful.

Ears are burning

Meaning talking about a person in his/her absence.

Examples We talked about Anil quite a bit. His ears must have been burning.

Your father was complaining about you yesterday. Were your ears burning?

Origin The Romans believed that when people talked about you in your absence, your ears tingled or burned. If the people in question were saying nice things about you, then it was the right ear that tingled. If, on the other hand, they were saying uncomplimentary things, then your left ear burned.

Eat crow

Meaning
to be humiliated; to eat humble pie. To admit that one is wrong, and take back what one has said.

Examples
After my team lost the game, I was made to eat crow.

If your plan doesn't click, you will be made to eat crow.

Origin
The expression is considered slang and is mostly used in American English. Most scholars believe that it is based on a true incident. According to the story, a British officer captured a hunter who had just shot a crow. In order to humiliate him, the officer made the poor man eat a small portion of the bird. When the gun was returned to him, the hunter turned it on the Englishman, and made him eat what was left of the crow!

Eat humble pie

Meaning
to act humbly after being proven that one was wrong about something.

Examples
After losing the elections, he was made to eat humble pie.

I am not saying anything now. I don't want to end up eating humble pie.

Origin The pie in the original expression was 'umble pie', and not 'humble pie'. The 'umbles' consisted of meat from the heart, liver and gizzard of the deer. It was usually the servants who ate these portions because they were not considered to be the choicest meat. Therefore, a person who ate 'umble pie' was one of low status.

Eat out of one's hand

Meaning to succeed in getting someone to do whatever you want; to have complete control of an individual.

Examples Within no time, the former film star had all the office employees eating out of her hand.

As a young man, Sameer dreamed he would have his wife eating out of his hand.

Origin The expression comes from the world of animal training. You know that a wild animal has been tamed when you succeed in getting it to eat something off your hands without getting bitten.

Egg on one's face

Meaning made to look foolish or feel embarrassed.

Examples Nikhil went around saying he would win the tournament. He lost in the first round. He has egg on his face.

Prem's fianceé ran away a week before their wedding. The poor chap has egg on his face.

Origin If you had an egg splattered all over your face, you would look pretty silly, wouldn't you?

Egghead

Meaning someone who has his head in the clouds; an intellectual, more interested in theory and abstract ideas rather than finding practical solutions to problems.

Examples I don't want an egghead like Radha on the committee.

Asking reporters to interview an egghead like Sam wasn't a very good idea.

Origin The word was first used to refer to bald men. Around 1918, journalists in Chicago started using it to mean 'intellectual'. The word became popular in the 1950s when Stewart Alsop, a newspaper columnist, and Richard Nixon, the Vice Presidential candidate for the Republican party accused the nominee of the Democratic party, Adlai Stevenson, of being an egghead: meaning that the candidate was out of touch with ordinary people and lacked the common sense to solve their problems.

Elephant in the room

Meaning a serious problem that everyone is aware of, but chooses to ignore. People try not to talk about it.

Examples Corruption is the elephant in the room that no politician is willing to talk about.

Plagiarism is an elephant in the room that no academic wishes to discuss.

Origin If an elephant were standing in your room, it would be impossible to ignore. Another expression which has the same meaning is 'gorilla in the room'.

Err on the side of caution

Meaning to decide to play it safe; to avoid taking too big a risk.

Examples Amarnath didn't take the threatening letters seriously. His wife, however, erred on the side of caution and informed the police.

Sailaja decided to err on the side of caution, and invested only twenty thousand in the company.

Even Homer nods/Homer sometimes nods

Meaning nobody is perfect.

Examples When I told Anjali there were a couple of errors in her report, she replied that Homer sometimes nods.

Aziz has been doing a brilliant job, but every now and then, he slips up. Even Homer nods, I guess.

Origin Homer is the Greek poet who wrote two great epics: *The Iliad* and *The Odyssey*. The word 'nod' in this context means to 'fall asleep'; even someone as great as Homer ended up making mistakes in his two epics because he had nodded off while writing. The idiom is actually a translation of a line from the Roman poet Horace, who in his *Ars Poetica*, wrote: "I think it is a shame when the worthy Homer nods: but in so long a work, it is allowable if drowsiness comes on."

Everything but the kitchen sink

Meaning used in informal contexts to mean 'everything imaginable'.

Examples It was the first time Nalini was travelling with the baby. She packed everything but the kitchen sink.

During her shopping spree in Paris, Leena bought everything but the kitchen sink.

Excuse/Pardon my French

Meaning an apology for swearing.

Examples I'll tell you what I think of the new Manager. Ladies, you'll have to pardon my French.

I've a lot of things to say. The delicate ones among you will have to excuse my French.

Origin The English hated the French; they thought that the French were people who swore all the time. Therefore, when an Englishman says, 'pardon my French,' what he means is that he is going to be using abusive language.

Eyes in the back of the head

Meaning being aware of everything that is happening around you; to sense everything.

Examples If you're the parent of a small child, you'll definitely have eyes in the back of your head.

Unfortunately, Tarun doesn't have eyes in the back of his head. He's clueless about what's happening in the company.

Face in the crowd

Meaning: to go unnoticed; one among the many.

Examples: Narender hates attending big parties. He doesn't like being a face in the crowd.

When the superstar arrived, the other actors became mere faces in the crowd.

Origin: When there are a lot of people and there is nothing about you which makes you stand out, then you are just a face in the crowd. It is what happens to most of us when we go to the stadium to watch a one-day international; we become a face in the crowd.

Face the music

Meaning: to face the consequences of one's action; to be punished.

Examples: If you don't finish this job by tomorrow, you'll face the music.

The children faced the music when their father got home.

Origin: When a soldier was dismissed from the army for dishonourable conduct, he was made to stand in front of the entire platoon. As the drums began to beat, an officer read out the crimes of the erring soldier; this was followed by the ripping out of the various insignias from his uniform. With the drums still beating, the soldier was ordered to leave the army premises.

Fag end

Meaning mostly used in informal contexts in British English to refer to the last part of something; very often, the most boring or the least important/ interesting part of something.

Examples Irfan began to bowl well only towards the fag end of the season.

Vittal walked in at the fag end of my presentaton.

Origin The word 'fag' in the expression refers to the frayed end of a rope or a piece of cloth – i.e., a rope or cloth which is worn out along the edges. In England, the word 'fag' is used to refer to 'cigarettes'. Initially, it was used to refer to 'cheap cigarettes'; later on, to cigarettes in general.

Fall like ninepins

Meaning being overcome very quickly: dying, falling or becoming ill very quickly. It is also possible to say 'drop like ninepins'.

Examples On the last day of the test match, the batsmen fell like ninepins.

If this disease spreads, people will drop like ninepins.

Origin ‘Ninepins’, also called ‘skittles’, is the name of a game. The aim of this game is to knock down nine bottle-shaped objects (ninepins) by rolling a ball at them. The expression is mainly used in British English.

Fall on stony ground

Meaning advice which one chooses to ignore.

Examples The Management’s repeated requests to call off the strike fell on stony ground.

I warned Harish about Geetha, but it looks like my warnings fell on stony ground.

Origin The person getting the advice is being compared to a ground that is so hard that nothing penetrates it. The expression comes from the *Bible*, and it has more or less the same meaning as ‘fall on deaf ears’.

Faustian bargain

Meaning a bargain made for temporary gain without taking into consideration future consequences; one that ultimately results in a person’s ruin. A much more common expression used nowadays is ‘make a pact/deal with the devil’.

Examples In order to win the elections, our leader has made a Faustian bargain with some of the extreme right-wing parties.

When the superstar was strapped for cash, he made a Faustian bargain with the Don of a drug cartel.

Origin According to most stories, Faust was a German scholar who was rather unhappy with his lot in life. The devil, Mephistopheles, appears and promises him that in return for his soul, he will give Faust unlimited power and knowledge. The greedy scholar signs on the dotted line and experiences all the worldly pleasures, but in the process, condemns his soul to hell.

Feather in one's cap

Meaning an achievement; an honour one can be proud of.

Examples Getting ten orders in a single day was a feather in the salesman's cap.

Winning five medals in the competition was a feather in Mahidhar's cap.

Origin In the old days, it was standard practice among soldiers to add a feather to their cap when they killed an enemy in battle. This tradition was followed by certain Native American tribes as well.

Feeling blue

Meaning — to feel sad or depressed.

Examples — After the farewell party, I was feeling blue.

I can't figure out why I'm feeling so blue this morning.

Origin — The 'blue' in the idiom has nothing to do with the colour; it refers to a type of music made popular by African Americans. 'Blues music' deals with rather sad themes, and as a result, leaves the listener feeling sad. Hence, the expressions 'to have the blues' and 'feeling blue' began to mean 'feeling sad or depressed'.

Fifth column

Meaning — a group of people who work against the country they are living in. Nowadays, the term is also used to refer to someone who is a traitor or a spy within an organisation. Every person belonging to such a column is called a 'fifth columnist'. The expression has a negative connotation.

Examples — The Government views some of the organisations in Kashmir as a fifth column – very likely to join forces with Pakistan soon.

Sushil believes there's a fifth column within the company, determined to ruin it.

Origin The expression was first used during the Spanish Civil War that took place between 1936 and 1939. According to some scholars, the term was coined by Queipo de Llano, a Lieutenant General in the rebel army. During one of his radio broadcasts, he claimed that the rebel army consisting of four columns would be marching on the city of Madrid. He said, "We have four columns on the battlefield against you and a fifth column inside your ranks." The expression became popular in English thanks to Ernest Hemingway's play, *The Fifth Column*.

Final nail in the coffin

Meaning the end of something; an event that causes harm or helps bring about the downfall of something or someone.

Examples Calling his new boss an idiot was the final nail in my friend's coffin.

The report in the newspaper is another nail in the coffin of the corrupt Minister.

Origin A coffin, as you know, is something that people are buried in. In the old days, the lid had to be nailed shut. The act of hammering in the final nail signified that the body inside was ready to be buried. It signified the end of one's existence on this planet.

Find one's feet

Meaning — become comfortable with what you are doing; establish yourself in a new place.

Examples — When I joined the company, my boss said that I would need time to learn about how the company works. He said I would find my feet gradually.

When Suchitra went to the States, she was miserable. But when she called us up last week, she said she was finally beginning to find her feet.

Origin — When a newborn animal begins to walk, its first steps are rather shaky. It takes some time for the animal to find its feet – to become sure-footed and walk without wobbles.

Fine-tooth comb

Meaning — a comb which has teeth very close together. When you go through something with a fine-tooth comb, you study it carefully or examine it in great detail.

Examples — When her earrings went missing, Hema went through her cupboard with a fine-tooth comb. She managed to find them.

The police realise that it's an important case. They've been going through the evidence with a fine-tooth comb.

Origin This is the kind of comb that is used to remove lice from an individual's hair.

Firing on all cylinders

Meaning working at full strength; operating as powerfully and effectively as possible.

Examples Ever since Gupta became the captain, his club has been firing on all cylinders.

Sajida is firing on all cylinders because she wants to finish the project tonight.

Origin The idiom refers to a well-oiled machine in which all the powerful cylinders are working effectively.

Fish in troubled waters

Meaning involving oneself in a dangerous situation in the hope of gaining some personal advantage; hoping to capitalise on someone else's misfortune.

Examples Bela is fishing in troubled waters by buying shares of that software company. I understand that the company is likely to go belly up.

Any country that interferes in Middle East politics is fishing in troubled waters.

Origin Fishermen believe that it is easy to catch fish when the water is 'troubled' or rough. Some believe that the fish come to the surface at this time, and therefore it is easier to catch them. Others argue that fish do not 'bite' any better in bad weather than in good weather. They claim that the bad weather drives away most fishermen, and as a result, the few that remain catch more fish.

Fits and starts

Meaning an activity which you start doing, stop after some time, and then resume again. Something that is not done regularly. It is possible to say 'in fits and starts' or 'by fits and starts'.

Examples It is going to take longer than expected. Work is progressing in fits and starts.

The response to our questionnaire is arriving by fits and starts.

Origin The expression has been around since the 1500s, and when it was first used, it was 'by fits'. 'Fits' in the context of the idiom referred to the strong emotion that people were sometimes overcome by – sorrow, joy, anger, etc. It was only in the 1600s that 'and starts' was added to the idiom.

Flog a dead horse

Meaning wasting one's time or effort trying to do something that is impossible; to talk about things that no one is interested in anymore.

Examples Dilshan is asking for more funding for his project. I think he's flogging a dead horse.

Talking about honesty to a bunch of politicians! That's what I call flogging a dead horse.

Origin Beating a horse that is already dead is a waste of one's time.

Flotsam and jetsam

Meaning useless and unimportant. The expression is normally used to refer to people without homes and jobs.

Examples The beggar was sharing the pavement with various other human flotsam and jetsam.

According to this report, teachers must make an effort to talk to the flotsam and jetsam – the students that the system is failing.

Origin This was originally an expression used by sailors. 'Flotsam' refers to the floating wreckage of a ship and its cargo. 'Jetsam', on the other hand, refers to cargo deliberately thrown overboard in order to lighten a ship during an emergency.

Fly-by-night operators

Meaning irresponsible, untrustworthy; businessmen who run away with the investors' money.

Examples There are many fly-by-night operators doing business.

You shouldn't have dealings with a fly-by-night company.

Origin Some people set up a company, do roaring business for about six months, and then disappear with everyone's money. The word 'fly' in the expression means 'to flee'. Since the shady characters who run such businesses leave town during the dead of night when everyone else is sound asleep, they are called 'fly-by-night' operators. The expression can be used with people and organisations.

Fly off the handle

Meaning to lose one's temper; to become extremely angry and shout.

Examples Our coach flies off the handle every time someone makes a mistake.

The CEO flew off the handle when he heard that the workers were going on strike.

Origin In the old days, axes were made by hand; sometimes, the axe head and the wooden handle were crudely fitted together. When people were cutting trees, it was quite common for the axe head to come loose and fly off its handle. The flying axe head used to cause a great deal of commotion among those working nearby. They let off steam by shouting at the person using the axe, or by cursing the implement itself.

Fools rush in where angels fear to tread

Meaning — inexperienced or ignorant people often do things without thinking matters through. They end up doing things which experienced people would avoid.

Examples — Chetan tried to settle the argument between Sailaja and Shilpa. You know what they say, fools rush in where angels fear to tread.

Mukund was keen on becoming the President of the club. Now he feels he shouldn't have contested. Fools rush in where angels fear to tread.

Origin — The expression is a creation of Alexander Pope, an English poet and essayist who lived in the 18th century. The line is found in his *Essay on Criticism*, and the fools that Pope is referring to are the literary critics of the period!

Foot the bill

Meaning — to pay the bill; to pick up the tab.

Examples I'm willing to come along if you promise to foot the bill.

If you think I'm going to foot the bill, you're out of your mind.

Origin The 'foot' in the expression has nothing to do with our feet. In the 15th century, when a waiter asked you to 'foot the bill', what he wanted you to do was to add up the figures and make sure that the total at the bottom or the foot of the bill was correct. The expression 'foot up', which is no longer in use, meant to 'count' or 'add up'. It was only in the 19th century that the expression 'foot the bill' began to mean what it does today.

Get down to brass tacks

Meaning to talk about the essentials, the basic facts of a particular situation.

Examples Let's get down to brass tacks. Who is going to pay for the broken window?

The General got down to brass tacks. He wanted to know how many soldiers had been posted along the border.

Origin Several explanations have been provided by scholars as to the origin of this expression. Some say that in Cockney, a dialect spoken in London, 'brass tacks' is rhyming slang for 'facts'. So when you said 'Let's get down to brass tacks', you meant 'Let's get down to the facts'. Another explanation is that in the old days, shopkeepers used brass tacks to measure the length of a piece of cloth. Merchants who sold material often had two brass tacks nailed on top of the counter. The distance between the two tacks was one yard. So when a customer wanted to know the length of a piece of cloth that he/she was interested in, the shopkeeper 'got down to brass tacks'. He used the tacks to determine the length of the cloth.

Get in someone's hair

Meaning — to bother or irritate a person; a source of nuisance.

Examples — I have the knack of getting in my boss' hair.

When Rashmi was young, she used to get in the Principal's hair.

Origin — What is the one thing that you do not want getting in your hair? Lice! When they manage to get in, they create all kinds of problems.

Get it in the neck

Meaning — to be punished or criticised.

Examples — Chalapthi got it in the neck for being late this morning.

The Registrar is likely to get it in the neck soon.

Origin In the old days, when someone was given capital punishment, his head was chopped off at the neck.

Get on the soapbox

Meaning to talk repeatedly about something one feels very strongly about; something which the listener has heard many times.

Examples Raju got on the soapbox and started telling the children about the evils of smoking.

Please don't get on the soapbox and tell us about the benefits of family planning.

Origin In the old days, when people wished to make a speech in a place of public gathering, they usually stood on a wooden box so that everyone in the audience could see them. This wooden box was called a 'soapbox', and anyone who got on the soapbox usually talked about something that he felt very strongly about. Such people were called 'soapbox orators'.

Get one's head out of the clouds

Meaning advising someone to be more realistic, to stop daydreaming.

Examples When I was young, my teacher told me that if I wanted to succeed, I needed to get my head out of the clouds.

It's really difficult to talk to Abhay. His head is always in the clouds.

Origin A person who has his head in the clouds will be unable to see the ground below; the air in the clouds will be so rarefied, the individual will become lightheaded and lose touch with reality.

Get someone's goat

Meaning to succeed in annoying an individual or in making him rather angry.

Examples Sometimes, Raja comes to work in jeans and T-shirt. It really gets my goat.

Kunal's constant whining gets my goat.

Origin The idiom comes from the world of horse racing. Horses are highly temperamental creatures, and in order to keep their prized possession calm and relaxed, trainers often kept a goat as a stable companion for the animal. Goats do not get flustered very easily, and their presence had a calming influence on the horse. Very often, the horse became rather attached to its little companion. To make sure that a particular horse did not perform well in a big race, stable boys working for rival owners sometimes stole the

Help! Someone's got my goat.

goat the night before the big event. The absence of its little friend made the horse moody, and as a result, it underperformed in the race. So when you say that someone has got your goat, you are comparing yourself to the horse, and not the goat.

Get the walking papers

Meaning to get the sack; to be fired.

Examples About fifty people were given their walking papers today.

After Sushmita got her walking papers, she started her own company.

Origin — The 'walking papers' is the letter from the company/boss informing you that your services are no longer required. You no longer need to be present on the premises; you can walk away and look for a job elsewhere.

Get to the bottom of something

Meaning — to spend time on a problem in order to find out the truth about it.

Examples — The investigators need to get to the bottom of this fraud.

There was something wrong, and the students wanted the Vice Chancellor to get to the bottom of it.

Origin — In order to get to something which is at the bottom, one has to remove everything that is at the top, and this takes time. In the process, we end up uncovering many things.

Get up on the wrong side of the bed

Meaning — to be in a bad mood for no obvious reason.

Examples — Prem is in a terrible mood. He must have got up on the wrong side of the bed.

Yesterday, my boss was shouting at everyone. He must have got up on the wrong side of the bed.

Origin The wrong side of the bed, in this context, refers to the left side of the bed. The Romans believed that the left side of anything was bad; if you got up on the left side, then chances were, you would be grumpy the whole day. All idioms which contain the word 'left' usually have a negative connotation: left-handed compliment, man with two left feet, etc. The word 'sinister' originally meant 'left handed'.

Get wind of something

Meaning to come to know about something; to acquire advance information.

Examples If Ram gets wind of what we're up to, we'll be in serious trouble.

The police got wind of a plot to assassinate the Chief Minister.

Origin Animals make use of their strong sense of smell to locate prey. They make use of the wind to do this; they are, very often, able to pinpoint the location of their potential prey even before they see them.

Get your act together

Meaning — to get organised; to do things in an effective manner.

Examples — My uncle is always telling my aunt to get her act together.

If you don't get your act together, you'll be spending the next year at home.

Origin — The expression comes from the world of theatre. In order to put on a good show, the various performers need to coordinate; they must learn to get their act together.

Ghost walks

Meaning — used in the world of theatre to mean 'payday'.

Examples — According to the Manager, the ghost walks today.

Will the ghost walk today?

Origin — The idiom is believed to have been coined in the 19th century. The story goes that the actors working for a small company had not received payment for several weeks. They were extremely angry about this, and decided to teach the producer a lesson. The play they were staging was Shakespeare's *Hamlet*. During one particular performance, Hamlet, waiting for his father's ghost to appear, said, "Perchance 'twill walk again." When he heard this, the actor playing the Ghost shouted from the wings: "No, I'll be damned if the ghost walks any more until our salaries are paid." According to the story, everyone received their salary that night!

Give a dog a bad/ill name and hang him

Meaning: once a person has acquired a bad reputation, it will stick with him the rest of his life.

Examples: Harish was arrested because there had been a burglary in his neighbourhood. The poor man wasn't even in town. I think it's a case of give a dog a bad name and hang him.

Nothing that Bharath does will convince Janaki that he is being honest with her. It's a case of give a dog an ill name and hang him.

Origin: You lose your reputation when people speak ill of you. "Reputation, reputation, reputation! O, I have lost my reputation! I have lost the immortal part of myself, and what remains is bestial." That is what Cassio says in Shakespeare's *Othello*. Once someone has lost his reputation, it is very difficult for the individual to regain it. When a person is caught stealing, he is forever branded a thief. Similarly, a dog that has acquired a bad reputation is branded for life. Another expression which has more or less the same meaning is 'he that has an ill name is half hanged.'

Give someone an even break

Meaning give a fair chance to someone; to be impartial.

Examples Sarita is very talented. All she needs is someone to give her an even break, and she could be at the top.

If you don't have a godfather, then no one will be willing to give you the even break you need to prove how good you are.

Origin There are several explanations for the origin of this expression. According to some scholars, it comes from the sport of dog racing. In the old days, it was common practice for people to take bets on whose dog was faster, and which one was better skilled at 'hare coursing'. In order to determine this, the owners held the animals tightly by the leash and released them at the same time. This letting go of the leash at the same moment – so that neither dog was at an advantage – was referred to as 'even break'. 'Hare coursing' was a bloody sport in which a poor hare was let loose, and the dogs were made to chase and kill the frightened animal.

Give someone the bird

Meaning to make fun of a performer; to hiss or boo him off stage.

Examples When Anjuman sang at the party, he got the bird from his friends.

The actor was given the bird when she forgot her lines.

Origin The original expression was 'to give the goose', and it was mainly used in the context of the theatre. Geese make hissing sounds when they are angry or feel threatened. When an actor did a bad job, he was hissed off stage. With the passage of time, 'goose' was replaced by 'bird'.

Give someone the cold shoulder

Meaning to ignore or reject someone; to make a person feel unwelcome.

Examples Some of the established stars have decided to give the press the cold shoulder.

When Uday fell from power, his friends gave him the cold shoulder.

Origin The meat from the 'shoulder' of mutton is tough and not very tasty. Centuries ago, this portion of mutton was usually given to the servants of the household. When guests came, the host made them feel welcome by providing them with good food. If, however, a guest overstayed his welcome, the servants were instructed to serve the visitor the 'shoulder' and that too 'cold'. On such occasions, the master did not make an appearance at the dining table. This was a hint to the visitor that it was time for him to move on.

Give someone the runaround

Meaning — to be evasive; to repeatedly avoid meeting someone.

Examples — Like most people, I hate it when someone gives me the runaround.

If you're not willing to grease palms, you'll get the runaround.

Origin — The idiom has been around for over a hundred years. The word 'runaround' means 'series of excuses, delays'. When you give the person who wishes to see you the runaround, you keep postponing or cancelling appointments for various reasons.

Give someone the third degree (see Third degree)

Give your eye teeth for something

Meaning: willing to do anything and go to any lengths to get something. The expression has more or less the same meaning as 'give your right arm for something'.

Examples: Most men would give their eye teeth to have Bhalla's rugged looks.

You are unhappy with your marks? I would give my eye teeth for them.

Origin: See 'Cut your eye teeth'.

Go bananas

Meaning: to behave in a slightly crazy or silly fashion.

Examples: The children will go bananas when they see the cute little puppy.

Divya went bananas when she heard that she had won the lottery.

Origin: Monkeys go crazy when they see bananas, their favourite fruit.

Go fly a kite

Meaning: to tell someone to get lost.

Examples: I told Raghu to go fly a kite.

You again? Why don't you go fly a kite?

Origin Serious-minded people do not waste their time flying kites. So, when you tell someone who is disturbing you to 'go fly a kite', you are implying that the person is capable of performing only such trivial tasks.

Go in one ear and out the other

Meaning information you soon forget.

Examples My friend's warning went in one ear and out the other.

Whenever my mother tells me something, it goes in one ear and out the other.

Origin Information which you consider unimportant enters through one ear and exits through the other. You do not retain it.

Go off the deep end

Meaning to become angry or hysterical; to overreact.

Examples Rajesh went off the deep end when he heard the workers were going on strike.

Prithi went off the deep end when she saw the mess the painters had made.

Origin The 'deep end' refers to the deep end of a swimming pool. When a person who does not know how to swim is thrown into the deep end, he splashes around frantically. He becomes hysterical.

Go south

Meaning used in informal contexts to mean 'to deteriorate or decline'.

Examples According to some experts, Djokovic's game has been heading south since the French Open.

My father and his friends are always saying that our country's economy is going south.

Origin On a map or a compass, we always associate 'south' with being 'down'.

Go to pot

Meaning to become run down; to go to ruin.

Examples My uncle believes that our politicians are responsible for letting this great country of ours go to pot.

It's sad to see many of our national monuments go to pot.

Origin The 'pot' refers to the vessel in which stew for the servants was made. During the Elizabethan period, servants threw inferior pieces of meat – ones that the master of the household did not wish to eat – into the pot. So, when a man said that he was going to pot, he meant that his status was going down in the world. He had come down to the level of his servants.

Go to someone's head

Meaning to make someone extremely proud or conceited.

Examples After scoring three centuries, Vivek let success go to his head.

Your new book is a big success, but don't let that go to your head.

Origin Success is being compared to drinking too much alcohol. When you consume too much alcohol, it goes to your head; sometimes, resulting in very odd behaviour.

Go/Come under the hammer

Meaning used to refer to objects that are on sale at a public auction. Nowadays, of course, even people 'go under the hammer'. In the IPL, for example, players come under the hammer every year.

Examples Some of Ravi Varma's paintings are going under the hammer next month.

The repossessed cars and motorcycles will be coming under the hammer next week.

Origin In a public auction, the person who is in charge of the event – the auctioneer – usually carries a wooden hammer with him. When the bidding for an article is over, he shouts 'sold' and hits the table with the hammer to indicate that the transaction has been completed.

Gobbledygook

Meaning a speech or piece of writing that is very complicated, and fails to make sense; gibberish.

Examples Whenever we asked a question, the answers came back in legal gobbledygook.

Talk to me in a language that I understand. I don't want any of your gobbledygook.

Origin 'Gobble' is the sound that a turkey makes. According to some scholars, the word 'gobbledygook' was coined by Congressman Maury Maverick. Apparently, he found the language used by officials unintelligible. He therefore issued the following memo: "Be short and say what you are talking about. Stop 'pointing up' programs. No more 'finalizing', 'effectuating', or 'dynamics'. Anyone using the words 'activation' or 'implementation' will be shot."

Pronunciation The 'o' in the first syllable is like the 'o' in 'cot', 'hot' and 'got'; the following 'e' is silent. The 'y' is pronounced like the 'i' in 'it', 'pit' and 'sit' and the final 'oo' sounds like the 'oo' in 'pool', 'cool' and 'tool'. The word is pronounced '**GO**-bl-di-gook', with the stress on the first syllable.

Good as it gets

Meaning the present situation is the best that one can hope for; things are not going to improve in any way.

Examples There is no point in shouting and getting upset. This is as good as it gets.

Don't have any expectations. This is as good as it gets.

Origin It is self explanatory.

Grapevine

Meaning gossip; information you hear from someone who, in turn, has heard it from someone else.

Examples I heard on the grapevine that Rohini is going to quit her job.

Mahesh heard through the grapevine that he was being promoted.

Origin According to one theory, the idiom came into existence when F B Morse came up with the idea of the telegraph. When Morse managed to send his message, "What hath God wrought", over the wire between Washington and Baltimore, many companies became interested in the telegraph. They competed with one another in putting up telegraph poles and lines. During the early years, the workmanship was very poor; the telegraph lines were not properly strung, and very often, they crisscrossed. The dangling wires reminded people of the crooked grapevine. Since information was being received through these wires, people came up with the expression 'through the grapevine'. As to why people began to believe that the information received through the grapevine was unreliable, we have to go back to the American Civil War that took place between 1861 and 1865. During this period, military commanders began to send battlefield reports in the form of telegrams. The enemy used to send a false report of the same battle; often, people were unsure about which report to believe. Therefore, anything heard through the grapevine was considered unreliable.

Greased lightning

Meaning — something/someone that/who moves very fast.

Examples — When Dhoni saw the Principal, he ran out the door like greased lightning.

Don't let the dented body fool you. This little car is greased lightning.

Origin — Grease is a lubricant that we frequently apply to machinery so that it runs smoothly. When a machine is greased, it runs faster and smoother. So what would happen if lightning were to be greased? It would strike even faster!

Green room

Meaning — room in a theatre where actors rest during a play.

Examples — I am sorry, but no one is allowed to enter the green room.

The green room is going to get a fresh coat of paint.

Origin — It was given this name because the walls in this room were traditionally painted green. People felt that 'green' was a soothing colour for the eyes. Since actors were exposed to harsh lights while on stage, they were provided something soothing to rest their eyes on. Nowadays, of course, the green room is not always painted green.

Green with envy

Meaning — to be jealous of someone or something.

Examples — When he saw Nikitha's new house, Aravind turned green with envy.

You don't have to turn green with envy. You're getting a promotion as well.

Origin The Greeks believed that when an individual became jealous, his system began producing too much bile. As a result, the complexion of the person turned yellowish green. This idea was made popular in 7 BC by the poet Sappho, when she used the word 'green' to describe the face of a jealous lover. With the passage of time, all poets began to associate 'green' with jealousy. Shakespeare immortalised the idea in *Othello*; talking about jealousy, the arch villain, Iago, says: "It is the green-eyed monster that doth mock the meat it feeds on."

Greenhorn

Meaning an inexperienced or naïve person; someone who can be easily duped or cheated.

Examples How could you give such an important assignment to a greenhorn?

The old man was looking for a greenhorn to whom he could sell his stocks.

Origin Before they harden, the horns of young animals are usually green in colour. The term was first used in the 15th century to refer to a young ox whose horns had not matured. Around the 17th century, the expression began to be used with people; any inexperienced person began to be called 'greenhorn'.

Grinning like a Cheshire cat

Meaning having a broad smile on one's face.

Examples Divya obviously knows something. She has been grinning like a Cheshire cat all morning.

When Leya walked in grinning like a Cheshire cat, I knew that she had come first in class.

Origin Cheshire is the name of a county in England which was once famous for its cheese. The cheese makers from this place used to draw the figure of a smiling cat on a special variety of cheese. So the cat in the idiom is not a real cat, but the image that was found on the cheese. Although the idiom had been around for several centuries, it was Lewis Carroll, the author of *Alice in Wonderland*, who made it famous. In the novel, Alice runs into a large cat with a big smile. When Alice asks why he is grinning, the Duchess replies, "It's a Cheshire cat and that's why."

Pronunciation The 'ch' is like the 'ch' in 'cheese', 'cheap' and 'chit'. The 'e' is like the 'e' in 'wet', 'set' and 'met', while the following 'sh' sounds like the 'sh' in 'sheep', 'ship' and 'shape'. The final 'ire' is pronounced like the 'a' in 'china'. The word is pronounced '**CHESH**-e', with the stress on the first syllable.

Grow on someone

Meaning to like someone or something we were not favourably disposed to in the beginning.

Examples The first time I heard the song, I didn't like it. Now it's beginning to grow on me.

I have a feeling that Debasmita will grow on you.

Origin We are not usually aware of a plant's growth: it is imperceptible.

Hair of the dog that bit someone

Meaning to overcome a hangover by having another drink.

Examples The headache is getting worse. I think I need some of the hair of the dog that bit me.

Here, drink this. It's the hair of the dog that bit you.

Origin In the old days, people believed that if you were bitten by a mad dog, the best antidote was to place hair from the animal's tail on the wound!

Hammer and tongs

Meaning to fight or argue with someone with a lot of energy and force; to do something with enthusiasm.

Examples — I wouldn't go in if I were you. Ramesh and Sujatha are going at it hammer and tongs.

It was a great game to watch. The two teams kept going at each other hammer and tongs till the very end.

Origin — The hammer and the tongs were tools generally used by a blacksmith. We all know what a hammer is; tongs was the instrument which the blacksmith used to remove red hot metal from thc firc and placc it on the anvil. The blacksmith held the metal down with the help of the long tongs and beat the hot metal into shape with the hammer. Since this activity involved a lot of vigorous hitting, the expression 'to go hammer and tongs' began to be used to refer to any activity where an individual went after something or someone vigorously.

Hand in glove

Meaning — to be closely involved with another individual, usually in an illegal activity; to be up to no good.

Examples — Some of the politicians were hand in glove with the militants.

I wouldn't trust anything Jai says. He's hand in glove with the Management.

Origin — The expression began to be used in the late 17th century. When first used, it was 'hand and glove', but later changed to 'hand in glove'. The expression is self explanatory. When your hand is inside the glove, the two are very close together, almost inseparable.

Handsome is as handsome does

Meaning good behaviour and chivalrous deeds are much more important than good looks.

Examples Venu may not be much to look at, but he is always helping those who are in need. Handsome is as handsome does.

Eshwar thinks he can get girls to do anything for him because of his good looks. He must realise that handsome is as handsome does.

Origin The expression has been around for several hundred years, and it has the same meaning as 'pretty is as pretty does'. According to some scholars, the expression was first recorded by the English poet, Geoffrey Chaucer.

Hang up one's boots

Meaning to call it a day; to retire. Other expressions which have the same meaning are 'hang up one's spikes' and 'hang up the gloves'.

Examples Rehman informed his adoring fans that he was planning to hang up his boots at the end of the season.

Don't you think it's time to hang up your boots, Priya?

Origin The expression was first used in football. When a player retires, he does not require his footwear or boots anymore. He can hang or suspend them from a nail or a peg.

Hangdog expression

Meaning an expression on someone's face which suggests that he is ashamed of what he has done.

Examples When Kanthi was arrested, she had a hangdog expression about her.

Vani sat opposite the Chairman with a gloomy hangdog expression.

Origin In medieval times, it was common practice among Europeans to put not only human beings on trial, but also animals. Whenever an animal did something wrong, it was put on trial, and if found guilty, it was sentenced to die by 'hanging'. If a dog bit a man and he died of rabies, the dog was put on trial for murder. In 1487, in France, beetles were formally charged for destroying a vineyard! The expression 'hangdog' was initially used to describe the look on the face of a person who was considered fit to be hanged like a dog for his crimes. Nowadays, the word is used to mean 'shamefaced'.

Happy as a clam

Meaning — to be extremely happy or delighted. Shorter form of the expression, 'happy as a clam at high tide'.

Examples — Jai was happy as a clam at high tide when he got the promotion.

Raj was happy as a clam when he heard the test had been postponed.

Origin — A clam is a sea creature that buries itself in the sand to escape predators. It has a shell that it uses to protect itself; when threatened, the two halves of the shell quickly snap shut. It is from this that we get the expression 'to clam up', to mean 'to stop talking' or 'refuse to talk'. Some varieties of clams are found very close to the seashore, and the best time to dig for them is when the tide – water level – is low. A clam becomes vulnerable during low tide. When the tide is high, it feels less threatened, and therefore much happier.

Hard to swallow

Meaning — to accept an unpleasant truth with difficulty.

Examples When I heard that Rajdeep had run away with the official documents, I found it hard to swallow.

When my sworn enemy was made my boss, it was hard to swallow.

Origin In the context of the idiom, 'hard' means 'bitter'. It is difficult to swallow something that is bitter.

Hat trick

Meaning achieving something three times in a short period. In cricket, taking three wickets in three balls. In football, scoring three goals in a game.

Examples In 1982, Chethan Sharma took a hat trick against New Zealand.

Ronaldo's latest hat trick helped his club win the championship.

Origin The term was first used in cricket. Nowadays, whenever a bowler performs a hat trick, he is given lots of money – either by the Board or by some sponsor. In the old days, when a bowler performed the 'trick' of getting three wickets off three balls, he got a new hat!

Hats off to someone

Meaning expressing admiration for someone.

Examples Hats off to the local administrator for managing to complete the job on time.

Hats off to Veda – it takes a lot of courage to learn music at 60.

Origin This is an expression that has been around since the 19th century. In the old days, when wearing hats was common, men showed their respect for someone, either by taking their hat off or by tipping their hat.

Haul someone over the coals

Meaning to criticise or reprimand someone severely. Americans tend to say 'rake someone over the coals'.

Examples My boss hauled me over the coals for showing up late for the meeting.

Runa raked her husband over the coals for forgetting her birthday.

Origin Raking someone over the coals was something that was common in Europe a few centuries ago. If people suspected that you were practising witchcraft, or that you did not believe in the teachings of the church, you were accused of being a heretic and dragged over red-hot coals. If you survived the ordeal, then you were declared innocent. If you did not, well it was just too bad.

Have a field day

Meaning used in informal contexts to mean 'to have a really good time'; to really enjoy oneself doing things that one likes to.

Examples If the media come to know about this scandal, they will have a field day.

Most of the teachers were absent, so the students had a field day at school.

Origin In the past, the term 'field day' was used to refer to the day when the army carried out manoeuvres or exercises on the field. Later, it began to be applied to the sports day celebrated in schools. With the passage of time, the term began to be applied to any fun activity – when people got together and enjoyed themselves.

Have/Got the runs

Meaning to have diarrhoea.

Examples Meera has lost a lot of weight. She's had the runs for over ten days now.

Everyone in Anshuman's family has got the runs.

Origin When people have a really bad upset stomach, they are frequently seen rushing or running to the bathroom; hence the expression, 'the runs'.

He who pays the piper calls the tune

Meaning — the person who provides the money for something has the right to decide how things should be done.

Examples — I don't agree with Jayachandran at all, but he's funding the project. He who pays the piper calls the tune.

The owner of the team has the right to decide who will play in the next match. He who pays the piper calls the tune.

Origin — In the old days, it was the job of the piper to provide music at various ceremonies. The kind of music he played depended on who was paying him. The piper played whatever music the person who was paying wanted him to.

High and dry

Meaning — used in informal contexts to mean 'to leave someone stranded; to desert someone in their time of need'. Another expression that has more or less the same meaning is 'leave someone in the lurch'.

Examples — When they sensed trouble, Tarun's partners resigned and left him high and dry.

The transport strike has left thousands of commuters high and dry.

Origin The expression was originally used to refer to a ship that had run aground – in other words, a vessel that had come too close to shore and got stuck in the sandy bottom. When this happened, the ship was said to be 'high' – since most of the vessel was out of the water, there was a lot more of the ship to see. It looked a lot 'taller' than when it was floating. The 'dry' in the expression refers to the bottom of the ship; a portion that is usually wet but which is now dry. A ship that was left high and dry was in a vulnerable position. There was nothing that the captain could do except wait for the high tide to come in.

Hightail it

Meaning to flee or leave a place quickly; to take to your heels. The expression is frequently used in informal contexts in American English.

Examples When I heard that Promod was coming, I hightailed it out of there.

Naveen hightailed it out of the house as soon as he got the call from his father.

Origin Many animals run when they sense they are in danger. Some animals, like rabbits, deer and horses, raise their tail high when they flee.

Hit below the belt

Meaning being very unsporting; being extremely cruel or unfair. It is also possible to say 'aim below the belt'.

Examples During the campaign, both candidates kept hitting each other below the belt.

Be careful with Ajit. He doesn't think twice about hitting someone below the belt.

Origin The expression comes from the world of boxing. In this sport, it is illegal to hit the opponent below the belt (waist). If you do throw a punch below the belt, you may be disqualified or points may be deducted from you.

Hit the ground running

Meaning to be ready for action; to begin your new task immediately, without delay.

Examples The people you've hired have no experience. How can you expect them to hit the ground running?

During the campaign, the candidate promised to hit the ground running.

Origin According to some people, the expression refers to soldiers who are dropped into enemy territory. When they are parachuted behind enemy lines, the soldiers make sure they land on their feet, with their guns drawn, ready for action.

Hit the sack/hay

Meaning a rather informal way of saying you are going to bed.

Examples I've had a tiring day. I think I'm going to hit the sack early today.

You don't expect me to hit the hay so early, do you?

Origin During the Second World War, American soldiers started referring to their sleeping bag as 'sack'. 'Hit the sack' replaced the earlier expression 'hit the hay'. Why hay? In the old days, people who could not afford a bed used to sleep on a sack stuffed with hay. Before they lay down to sleep, they would keep hitting the sack till the straw/hay was evenly spread.

Hobson's choice

Meaning to have no choice at all; to take what is offered or get nothing at all.

Examples Venkatesh didn't really want to stay in that particular hotel, but it was a case of Hobson's choice. All the other hotels were full.

It's Hobson's choice because if I don't agree to do what my boss says, I'll definitely lose my job.

Origin Thomas Hobson (1544–1631) owned a stable in Cambridge, England, and rented horses to people who required them. He was a very methodical man, and insisted that all his horses be exercised in regular rotation. When a horse that had been rented was returned to him, it was placed at the end of the line. This was Hobson's way of ensuring that all his horses did an equal amount of work. The horse that was next in line to be rented was placed near the stable door. If the customer was not satisfied with the horse being offered, he was told to try his luck elsewhere. The customer had no choice in the matter; he could either 'take it or leave it'.

Hoist with one's own petard

Meaning to create problems for oneself.

Examples Shambu wanted to murder Ram but was hoisted with his own petard when he accidentally ate the poison that was intended for his younger brother.

The teachers were hoisted with their own petard when the inquiry they had asked for determined that they were being overpaid and not underpaid.

Origin Shakespeare used this expression in his tragedy, *Hamlet*. The 'petard' was actually a crude bomb used in the old days by invading armies. Soldiers used to place these bell-shaped bombs near the walls and gates of forts, and light a slow burning fuse. Sometimes, the fuse burnt much more quickly than expected, and in the process, blew up not only the walls and the gate, but also the man who had lit the fuse.

Pronunciation The 'e' in 'petard' can be pronounced like the 'a' in 'china' or like the 'i' in 'bit', 'kit' and 'fit'. The final 'ard' rhymes with the words 'card', 'bard' and 'hard'. The word is pronounced 'pi-**TARD**', with the stress on the second syllable.

Home away from home

Meaning to feel as comfortable and as relaxed somewhere as you do in your own home. The British prefer to say 'a home from home'.

Examples My brother-in-law visits Mumbai so often that it's become his home away from home.

Usha likes spending time with Sarita and her family. It's her home away from home.

Homeric laughter

Meaning: to laugh loudly and at times uncontrollably; it is usually prolonged, and the entire body shakes during the process.

Example: Peals of Homeric laughter rang out of the room where Pooja was performing.

Origin: The Homer referred to in this expression is the Greek poet and not the leading character from the well-known television show, *The Simpsons*. Belly-shaking laughter is called Homeric laughter because this is how the gods laughed in Homer's classics.

Hook, line and sinker

Meaning: to believe something completely; being gullible.

Examples: Shyam expected his students to swallow his explanation hook, line and sinker.

Vidya fell for the news channel's interpretation of the event hook, line and sinker.

Origin: The expression comes from the sport of fishing. Sometimes, a fish not only swallows the hook to which the bait is attached, but also some of the 'line'. The sinker is the weight that is used to take the fishing line to the bottom. It is, however, very uncommon for a fish to swallow the 'sinker'. So, if someone swallows your tall story hook, line and sinker, he/she is being very gullible.

(by) Hook or by crook

Meaning to be determined to do something, come what may, and not be worried about the consequences.

Examples Whenever you give Madhu a task, he gets it done by hook or by crook.

I have a deadline to meet. I'll meet it by hook or by crook.

Origin In medieval Britain, tenants were allowed to collect firewood from trees located on their landlord's property. To protect the trees and to ensure that they were not chopped down indiscriminately, there was a law which was strictly enforced. People were allowed to cut down only those branches which they could reach. The tenants were not allowed to climb a tree and chop off any of the branches at the top. To reach the branches that were high up, people started using 'hooks' and 'crooks'. A 'crook' was a long stick with a curved handle; the kind which shepherds used to carry in the old days. People used both the hooks and crooks to pull down the higher branches and chop them down. They got the branches by hook or by crook! The expression is considered old fashioned.

Horns of a dilemma

Meaning — to choose between two rather unpleasant options; no matter what you choose, you end up losing. The expression has more or less the same meaning as 'between the devil and the deep blue sea'.

Examples — If I sell the shares now, I won't make a profit. If I don't sell them, I won't be able to repay the loan. I'm on the horns of a dilemma.

Ganesh can't decide which player to drop. He's on the horns of a dilemma.

Origin — In a debate, when you present your opponent with a 'dilemma', you provide him with two choices. It does not matter which option he chooses to respond to because either way he will lose the argument; he is in a no-win situation. You are asking your opponent to choose between two horns of a bull, and whichever one he chooses, he is going to be gored.

Horse sense

Meaning — common sense.

Examples — Horse sense told me that I would be a fool to buy any of the shares that my cousin was trying to sell.

The new Vice Chancellor is not a great scholar, but he has enough horse sense to tackle everyday problems.

Origin This American expression comes from the Wild West. Cowboys believed that the animal they rode had a lot of common sense and therefore was incapable of doing anything stupid. It would not attempt to jump over something that it was incapable of or take a dangerous path. Also, some of the cow ponies that the cowboys rode did a wonderful job of herding cattle: they completed this task without their masters telling them what to do.

Horse-trading

Meaning shrewd bargaining. The two bargaining parties show an understanding of the problem and the negotiations are done in a hard and clever manner.

Examples If you want to do some horse-trading, you'd better take Venkat along.

The MLAs were involved in a lot of political horse-trading to arrive at a consensus candidate.

Origin The expression is mostly used to show disapproval. Nowadays, people are reluctant to trust a used-car salesman. In the past, horse traders had a similar reputation; they were well-known for their shrewd, but often shady, business deals.

Horses for courses

Meaning — choosing the person ideally suited for a particular job on hand. This individual may not be the best person on the team, but he has the required skills that you are looking for.

Examples — Lalitha was better qualified, but we were looking for someone who had lived abroad. It was horses for courses as far as we were concerned.

There are many good dictionaries in the market; choosing the right one is a matter of horses for courses.

Origin — The expression comes from the world of horse racing. Racing pundits believe that some horses are better suited for certain types of racetracks. Some horses run well on tracks that are wet, while others do well on dry tracks.

Hot on the heels of

Meaning — very close to someone you are pursuing or chasing. Chances are you will catch him or overtake him soon. Other expressions which have the same meaning are 'hard on the heels' and 'in hot pursuit'.

Examples The young detective was hot on the heels of the thief.

The challenger was hot on the heels of the champion.

Origin According to scholars, the word 'hot' has been used in the expression to suggest that the pursuer is on track; in other words, he is not lost, and the trail has not gone cold. He is so close to his prey that he is able to feel the 'heat' generated by the animal/individual.

Hot potato

Meaning a controversial or sensitive topic/subject that people are reluctant to talk about or deal with.

Examples In many countries, abortion continues to be a hot potato.

There was a time when the Mandal Commission Report was a political hot potato.

Origin See 'Drop like a hot potato'.

Hot under the collar

Meaning to get very angry.

Examples You could see that Vijay was getting hot under the collar.

Vishnu got hot under the collar when the teacher accused him of cheating.

Origin When we get angry, usually our body temperature rises; our face and neck feel hot, our palms sweat, etc. And where is our neck? It is usually under the collar!

I'm a Dutchman

Meaning exclamation of surprise; you don't believe what the person has said.

Examples Sujatha has got a hundred in her physics test! I'm a Dutchman.

Rama won the beauty pageant! I'm a Dutchman.

Origin English idioms containing the word 'Dutch' ('Dutch treat', 'Dutch courage', 'Dutch auction', 'double Dutch', etc.) are rather uncomplimentary. This is because the English did not particularly like the Dutch.

Icing on the cake

Meaning something that happens which makes your happy situation even better. It is also possible to say, 'frosting on the cake'.

Examples I was thrilled after winning my first title. When the person from Nike told me the company was going to sponsor me, it was icing on the cake.

Achala was very excited when her first book was published. When Sony Pictures offered to buy the movie rights, it was icing on the cake.

Origin Most people like eating cake. They enjoy it even more when the cake has icing on it. Some children take great delight in licking off the icing before they start eating the cake.

In Dutch

Meaning to be in trouble.

Examples I'm in Dutch with my boss.

Geetha is in Dutch with her parents for losing her bicycle.

Origin If one failed to do one's duty, one was given a talking to by the Dutch uncle. This person did not mince words; he was severe in his criticism.

In one's crosshairs

Meaning to become a person of interest; to have someone's sights trained on you.

Examples The spate of scandals has put most politicians in the crosshairs of journalists.

The hunter has had the tiger in the crosshairs for a long time.

Origin The crosshairs in the idiom refers to the two perpendicular lines you see when you view a target through the telescopic sight of a rifle. These lines help the shooter aim at the target.

In one's good books

Meaning to be in someone's good graces; the person likes you, and approves of you.

Examples Surabhi got the promotion because she is in the Chairman's good books.

I have been in Ashwin's good books ever since I helped him change his flat tyre.

Origin In the old days, people kept two books. In one book, they wrote down the names of people they liked, and in the other, the names of people they did not like.

In the doghouse

Meaning to be in disfavour; people are annoyed because of something the person has done.

Examples When a man forgets his wife's birthday, he's really in the doghouse.

My husband forgot my birthday! He is in the doghouse again.

Devdas is really in the doghouse. He was late for the appointment again.

Origin

When a dog misbehaves, it is often scolded, and as a form of punishment, is made to spend time in its kennel: away from the comfort of the master's home. Some scholars believe the expression comes from the well-known children's novel, *Peter Pan*. When Wendy and her brothers run away with Peter Pan to Never Never Land, Mr. Darling, the children's father, spends his time in the doghouse. He does this as a form of penance because he had tied up their dog, Nana, on the night the children flew away with Peter.

In the doldrums

Meaning in very low spirits; feeling depressed.

Examples Vinita is usually in the doldrums during the monsoon season.

The movie industry is in the doldrums.

Origin This expression comes from the world of sailing. In the old days, ships depended on the wind to get from one place to another. If there was no wind, the ship remained stagnant. 'Doldrums' is the name of a place situated near the equator where there is not much wind. Sometimes, ships floated around helplessly for several days or weeks in the region – till the wind filled the sails and helped them to move along. When sailors were caught in the doldrums, they felt bored and often became depressed. As time went by, the expression was used to refer to anyone who was feeling depressed.

In the groove

Meaning to be able to do something quite easily, without any real effort.

Examples When Federer returned in 2017, it took him time to get in the groove.

Anand didn't like being a Manager at first; but now, he's getting in the groove.

Origin A 'groove' is a long, thin cut on a hard surface. For example, sliding doors and windows have grooves cut into them. They make it possible for a person to slide the door/window easily. The groove in the expression refers to the groove found in the records that we used to play when we wished to listen to music.

Pronunciation The word rhymes with 'move' and 'prove'.

In the swim

Meaning to be actively participating in the things happening around you; to be in the 'thick of things'. The expression can also be used to mean 'to be up-to-date; someone who is well informed'. The opposite of this expression is 'out of the swim of things'.

Examples It took Sachi only one day to get in the swim of things.

If you want more information, talk to Ratna. She is in the swim.

Origin The 'swim' in the expression has nothing to do with the activity of swimming. The word, in fact, comes from the world of fishing. Fishermen, or anglers as they are sometimes called, use the word 'swim' to refer to the section of the lake/river where fish can be found in plenty.

In the wake of something

Meaning coming after something or as a consequence of something.

Examples The security at the temples and mosques has been extra tight in the wake of last week's bomb blasts.

The tsunami left a trail of destruction in its wake.

Origin The 'wake' has nothing to do with waking up from sleep. In this case, the word refers to the turbulence left by something moving through the water. In other words, the waves or path that a moving ship or boat leaves behind is a 'wake'.

Inside track

Meaning to be in a position where you are at an advantage.

Examples My boss has the inside track, so the chances are our company will get the contract.

Ganesh's boss has a really good opinion of him. Since he's got the inside track, chances are he will be promoted to Assistant Manager.

Origin The term 'inside track' refers to the first lane of a running track. Since this lane does not curve as much as the other lanes do, the individual running on this track is at an advantage.

Iron out the wrinkles

Meaning to smooth out or solve a problem.

Examples We sat down and managed to iron out the wrinkles pretty quickly.

We need to iron out a few wrinkles before we sign the contract.

Origin In this expression, the word 'wrinkles' refers to problems. When we iron clothes, we get rid of all the wrinkles in them!

Jack Robinson

Meaning to do something very quickly.

Examples Before I could say Jack Robinson, she shut the door.

The lion disappeared before anyone could say Jack Robinson.

Origin The complete expression is 'before you can say Jack Robinson' and it has been part of American slang for over two hundred years. No one is really sure who this man was. According to one story, Jack Robinson was a well-to-do gentleman who went around knocking on people's doors, and disappeared before they opened it.

Joined at the hip

Meaning to be inseparable; to always be together.

Examples Ramesh and Karthik have been joined at the hip since college.

I can go to Chennai without my cousin. We're not joined at the hip, you know.

Origin When two people are joined at the hip, like Siamese twins are, they are inseparable. They are always together.

Joker in the pack

Meaning an unknown entity; someone who is likely to have a big impact on the events that will follow. The results of the person's influence, however, will be hard to predict – they may be most unexpected.

Examples The young voter was the joker in the pack in the last election.

Don't say anything about abortion. It may be the joker in the pack that might help you win this election.

Origin The expression comes from the world of card games. In certain games, the joker can be assigned any value – it can be used as an Ace, a Jack, a King, etc. The value that a player will assign a joker cannot be predicted.

Kangaroo court

Meaning — a court of law where justice is not served; the legal rights of an individual are totally disregarded.

Examples — Sneha was sent to prison by a kangaroo court.

The author claims the panchayat is nothing more than a kangaroo court.

This court finds the defendant guilty.

Origin The original 'kangaroo court' was not a real court, but a mock one. It was set up by prisoners in large prisons to maintain order. Whenever a prisoner did something wrong, the other inmates decided the punishment that was to be handed out to the culprit. Needless to say, justice was not always served. The expression 'kangaroo court' tells you what the Americans thought of the justice system in Australia. Remember, the first people to be sent to the land of the kangaroo were mostly prisoners from England.

Pronunciation The first 'a' sounds like the 'a' in 'cat' and 'bat', while the second is like the 'a' in 'china'. The 'oo' sounds like the 'oo' in 'cool', 'pool' and 'fool'. The word is pronounced 'kan-ge-**ROO**', with the stress on the final syllable.

Keep a straight face

Meaning be expressionless; not laugh or smile.

Examples When my boss fell off his chair, I found it difficult to keep a straight face.

It was hard to keep a straight face when I was talking to Sujatha today.

Origin The word 'straight' in this context means expressionless. When we laugh or frown, our face changes, and it informs others as to the kind of mood we are in. The expression 'to keep a straight face' was first used in the game of cards.

A good player of poker keeps his face wooden; by doing this, he makes it difficult for the other players to know what kind of cards he is holding.

Keep a tight/short leash on someone

Meaning — to keep someone under control; to keep him under check. Not give too much freedom.

Examples — Our new boss is very strict. He has all of us on a tight leash.

Ever since Gopal got into trouble at school, his father has kept him on a short leash.

Origin — A leash is the rope or the long thin piece of leather strap that you put around an animal's neck – dog, cow, etc. – to keep it under control.

Keep it under your hat

Meaning — keep the information a secret.

Examples — Raja and Revathi are planning to elope. But keep it under your hat.

I have some interesting news. I'll tell you, if you promise to keep it under your hat

Origin — In the old days in Britain, both boys and men used to wear hats. Some of the hats had secret compartments in them. Whenever a man carried something important, he invariably hid it in them.

Sometimes, when a man wanted to send a letter to his beloved, he hired a small boy from the streets. The boy was given the letter and it was his job to give it to the girl without her parents being aware of it. In order to ensure that he did not lose the letter and was in a position to give it to the girl without her parents finding out, the boy used to keep it under his hat!

Keep one's chin up

Meaning to remain cheerful/positive under difficult circumstances.

Examples The players were devastated when they conceded the second goal. The coach told them to keep their chin up and keep fighting.

When Madhuri's first movie bombed at the box office, she didn't get depressed. She kept her chin up and worked really hard. Today, she's a superstar.

Origin When one is sad or when things do not go according to plan, one drops one's head – in the process, one drops one's chin as well.

Keep one's eyes peeled

Meaning to remain alert or watchful; to keep one's eyes open.

Examples — If you are planning to cut across the field, please keep your eyes peeled for stray dogs. They can be pretty vicious.

Keep your eyes peeled for Mahesh. He said he would be coming.

Origin — When you peel a fruit, you remove its skin or the outer covering. When you ask someone to keep his eyes peeled, you are asking him to remove everything that might block his vision. You are telling him not to close his eyelids.

Keep one's fingers crossed

Meaning — to hope or pray things will go according to plan.

Examples — We are keeping our fingers crossed and hoping it won't rain during the picnic.

Sushmita will win a million dollars if she answers the next question. Keep your fingers crossed.

Origin — The expression has been part of the English language for over a century. The two fingers that you cross are the middle finger and the pointer, often referred to as the 'index' finger. People believed when you made the sign of the cross in this manner, you kept bad luck away. The expression has more or less the same meaning as 'touch wood'.

Keep tabs on someone

Meaning — to monitor or keep track of what someone is doing. It is possible to use the expression with things as well.

Examples — I keep telling Sachi that she needs to keep tabs on her bank balance.

Raju feels that his wife is keeping tabs on his every move.

Origin — The expression was first used in America in the mid-19th century. According to some scholars, bartenders started using a slate to write down the number of drinks each customer had consumed. Another name for the slate was 'tablet', and it is from the shortened form of this word that we get 'tab'. Since the bartender had to watch each customer carefully to keep track of the number of drinks he had consumed, the expression 'keep tabs on' began to mean 'to monitor'.

Keep under wraps

Meaning — to keep something a secret.

Examples — The names of the people arrested during the sting operation are being kept under wraps.

Kshema plans to keep her engagement under wraps for a while.

Origin When you cover an object by wrapping it up, it becomes impossible for people to know what is inside. The object remains hidden.

Keep your powder dry

Meaning to remain calm and be ready for action.

Examples The soldiers were asked to keep their powder dry and await orders.

Don't panic, you understand? All I am asking you to do is to keep your powder dry.

Origin The powder in the idiom refers to gunpowder. In the old days, gunpowder and a steel ball had to be pushed down the barrel of a gun, before it could be fired. The powder had to remain dry for the gun to fire. People carrying guns made sure that the powder did not get wet. Sir Oliver Cromwell is believed to have coined this expression. Before crossing a river to attack his enemy, he told his troops: "Put your trust in God, but be sure to keep your powder dry."

Keep your shirt on

Meaning don't get angry, let's not fight. Wait a minute!

Examples The pizza isn't done yet. Just keep your shirt on, little fellow.

During the meeting, people may lose their cool. But you keep your shirt on.

Origin In the old days, the common man didn't have too many shirts. Whenever he got into a fight, he invariably removed his shirt, so that it did not get torn. When you tell someone to keep his shirt on, you are telling him that you are not interested in a fight.

Kick the bucket

Meaning to die.

Examples The greedy children are waiting for the old man to kick the bucket.

The shops are closed because the local MLA kicked the bucket last night.

Origin There are several explanations for the origin of this idiom. Some believe that several centuries ago, people made use of buckets to commit suicide. A man who wished to hang himself, used to turn the bucket upside down, stand on it and then proceed to put a noose around his neck. Once he had completed this task, he would then kick the bucket away. Result? Death, by hanging!

Kitchen cabinet

Meaning a small group of people that the Prime Minister or President of a country turns to for advice. These unofficial advisers are not politicians.

Example According to rumours, the PM's kitchen cabinet consists of just four people.

Origin The expression 'kitchen cabinet' was coined in the United States in the 1830s during the presidency of Andrew Jackson. He had three friends whom he depended on for advice. Since he wanted to keep their visits a secret, he usually had them ushered in through the kitchen door. It is believed that most of their meetings actually took place in the kitchen: hence the term 'kitchen cabinet'. Other expressions which have more or less the same meaning are 'brain(s) trust' and 'think tank'.

Knee high to a grasshopper

Meaning short and small.

Examples I haven't seen Ravi since he was knee high to a grasshopper.

My mother tells me when I was knee high to a grasshopper, I was really cute.

Origin A grasshopper is a relatively small insect. If you only come up to its knees, then you are really small. The idiom is an exaggerated way of saying that the person in question is short.

Knee-jerk response/reaction

Meaning doing something quickly and automatically, without thinking.

Examples When the politician was asked if he liked the PM, he said, 'Yes'. I think it was a knee-jerk response.

Every time I see Supriya, I wince. It's a knee-jerk reaction.

Origin In the old days, when someone went to a doctor, he was invariably tapped on the knee with a rubber hammer. When the doctor did this, the tapped leg shot up automatically; it was a spontaneous response with no thinking involved.

Knock the socks off

Meaning something that really pleased or excited you; blown away by the experience. Also possible to say 'blow the socks off '.

Examples You should see Narender's new car. It'll knock your socks off.

The new restaurant is a very small place. The decor isn't great, but the food will simply blow your socks off.

Origin — This is an example of how an idiom changes its meaning completely. The expression comes from the world of boxing, and originally, beating the socks off your opponent meant destroying him completely. You gave him such a thrashing that the man not only lost consciousness, but also his shoes and socks.

Know one's onions

Meaning — to be skilled or well informed.

Examples — The school has a reputation for hiring teachers who know their onions.

There is not one person in our office who knows his onions.

Origin — Some people believe the expression refers to C.T. Onions, the Editor of the *Oxford English Dictionary*. This, however, is not the case because the idiom is American in origin. No one is really sure about how this expression came into being. The only thing that scholars are certain about is that the Americans had several such idioms: 'know one's oats', 'know one's beans', 'know one's oil' and 'know one's apples'. Among these, 'know one's onions' became very popular.

Know which side the bread is buttered

Meaning — to know what is good for you; smart enough not to offend people in power.

Examples — Policemen don't take action against politicians because they know which side their bread is buttered.

Sajid didn't say anything against the Principal because he knew which side his bread was buttered.

Origin — The expression is based on a Yiddish folktale. According to the story, the people of Chelm, a city in Poland, were very stupid. One day someone dropped a slice of bread, and incredibly enough, it landed butter side up, instead of butter side down. The Wise Men of Chelm were asked why the slice had landed butter side up. After reflecting on the problem for a week, they concluded that the slice had been buttered on the wrong side!

Last but not least

Meaning — finally, but not less importantly; the person/ object is as important as the others.

Examples — I have put all the important items in the handbag. My ticket, my passport, my medicines, and last but not least, my iPod.

Last but not least, this is Suman.

Origin — The expression has been around since the 16th century and is self explanatory.

Laugh up your sleeve

Meaning — to laugh quietly or secretly, often contemptuously. When you do this, you are hiding your amusement; you are ridiculing the person.

Examples — Nagesh pretended to admire Sachu's paintings, but we knew he was laughing up his sleeve.

John looked very serious, but he was laughing up his sleeve at the terrible performance.

Origin — In the 16th century, it was fashionable for men to wear a shirt that had fluffy sleeves. The sleeves were so big that whenever an individual wanted to laugh secretly, he hid his face in them and laughed.

Lay someone out in lavender

Meaning — used in informal contexts to mean 'to criticise or scold someone severely'.

Examples — The CEO was angry with Madhavan. She laid him out in lavender.

When Suresh heard that the annual report was not ready, he really laid his Office Assistant out in lavender.

Origin The lavender flower is well known for its aroma. At funerals, this flower was placed close to the coffin in order to hide the smell of the body. In the past, in order to transfer the wonderful smell of the flower onto their clothes, ladies would beat their freshly washed laundry with the branches of the plant. The original meaning of 'lay someone out in lavender' was 'to beat a person till he became unconscious'. With the passage of time, the beating became more verbal than physical.

Lead someone down/up the garden path

Meaning to try to cheat or deceive someone.

Examples Latha told Pradeep that she loved him. What he didn't realise was that she was leading him down the garden path. She needed help with her project.

In most countries, it's the politicians who lead the people up the garden path.

Origin In the old days, it was common practice among young unmarried couples to take a stroll in the garden, hoping to find a secluded spot.

Learn the ropes

Meaning a beginner, someone learning how a particular job or task is done.

Examples Once I learn the ropes, my boss will take notice of me.

We had to let him go. Ravi couldn't learn the ropes.

Origin The expression comes from the world of sailing. In the old days, a sailor had to know his ropes: he needed to know how many ropes there were on the ship, what their functions were, and how they were arranged. He also needed to be an expert in tying various types of knots with the ropes.

Leave no stone unturned

Meaning to do everything possible to achieve something; to use every possible means to get the desired result.

Examples The Chief Minister has said that he would leave no stone unturned to find the culprit.

Both countries claimed they would leave no stone unturned to find peace.

Origin In 477 BC, General Polycrates defeated General Mardonius in battle. According to rumours, the Persian general, Mardonius, had hidden a lot of treasure in his tent. But when Polycrates and his men searched the tent, they found nothing. The disappointed General went to an oracle in Delphi and told him of his problem. The oracle instructed him to return to the place where the battle had been fought, and to look under every stone for the treasure; he asked him to leave no stone unturned. Polycrates went back, and searched under the stones, and sure enough, he found the treasure.

Leave someone cold

Meaning fail to excite or interest.

Examples Brad Pitt's performance in the movie left me cold.

All the candidates I listened to left me cold.

Origin In the past, people believed the temperature of the blood in the human body varied depending upon the mood the person was in. See 'Murder someone in cold blood'.

Leave someone holding the bag

Meaning to make someone the scapegoat; make him take all the blame for some wrong that you have done.

Examples It was the Minister's fault, but he wasn't the one left holding the bag.

When the window broke, everyone ran away. Mala was left holding the bag.

Origin The expression comes from the sport of bird hunting. In the old days, whenever a new boy moved into a neighbourhood, the other boys welcomed him by playing a trick on him. They used to take him to the woods at night to do some bird hunting. The new kid on the block was usually given a sack and a lantern to hold. When they had gone deep into the woods, the new boy was instructed to do two things: to keep the bag open and hold the lantern slightly above the bag. He was told that when they 'beat around the bush', the frightened birds would fly straight for the light and in the process get caught in the bag. As you have probably guessed by now, instead of going into the bush to scare the birds, the other boys went home; leaving the poor newcomer 'holding the bag'.

Left-handed compliment

Meaning — something that sounds like a compliment, but is, in fact, an insult or a criticism.

Examples — Sujatha takes delight in paying me left-handed compliments.

Das said I looked stunning in my torn jeans. I think he was paying me a left-handed compliment.

Origin — A 'left-handed compliment' means the same thing as a 'backhanded compliment'. Among Europeans, anything associated with the left side is bad. See 'Get up on the wrong side of the bed'.

Left holding the baby

Meaning to inconvenience someone or burden him with additional responsibility; to be made a scapegoat.

Examples When the company went bankrupt, all the partners ran away. My poor cousin was left holding the baby.

I want everything in writing. I certainly don't wish to be left holding the baby.

Origin Looking after a baby is a major responsibility. If the person who is supposed to be taking care of the baby, hands it over to you and does the disappearing act, you have a major problem.

Let one's hair down

Meaning to begin to relax and enjoy oneself; to tell someone what is on your mind.

Examples Come on, Kim, let your hair down, and tell me what's bothering you.

Gayathri really let her hair down at the party.

Origin In the old days, women with long hair usually put it up in a bun. They never let their hair down. The only time they actually did this was in the privacy of their bedroom. Therefore, when someone lets his/her hair down, it means he or she is being very informal.

Let someone cool their heels

Meaning — to keep someone waiting.

Examples — The Principal must have sensed that you are angry about something. That's why he is letting you cool your heels.

I let Atia cool her heels for a while before talking to her about the problem.

Origin — When you walk, your feet become warm. When you are made to wait or sit down, they cool down.

Let the cat out of the bag

Meaning — to reveal a secret accidentally.

Examples — Please don't tell Vinod anything. He'll let the cat out of the bag.

Sohan let the cat out of the bag when he said he had to buy a ring before meeting Radha.

Origin — In medieval times, pigs and piglets used to be sold in open markets and fairs. Since the seller did not want these animals running around, they were tied up, drugged and put in a sack. At times, a cunning seller would put a cat instead of a piglet inside the sack. When the unsuspecting buyer opened the bag at home, the truth was out: a cat was literally taken out of the bag! Another expression which has the same meaning is 'buy a pig in a poke'.

Let the chips fall where they may

Meaning do whatever you have to do without worrying too much about the consequences of your action. Do the right thing without worrying about the fallout.

Examples The Minister said that he would speak from the heart and let the chips fall where they may.

Venu decided he would tell his father the truth, and let the chips fall where they may.

Origin The 'chips' has nothing to do with the chips we normally eat. This American idiom comes from the world of logging. When you are trying to chop down a tree using an axe, every time you hit the tree, pieces of wood (chips) scatter. While you are cutting, you do not worry about the various chips flying around; you do not really care where they land. As a cutter, you remain focused on the task at hand – which is to chop down the tree.

Let the grass grow under one's feet

Meaning to be idle, to waste time.

Examples The Chairman let the grass grow under his feet. As a result, the project wasn't completed on time.

You can't let the grass grow under your feet. You have millions invested in this project.

Origin Grass grows slowly, and the only way it will grow under your feet is if you remain standing in one place for a long time.

Level best

Meaning to do whatever one can; to make the maximum effort.

Examples Prakash is doing his level best to solve the problem.

Our team did its level best to beat the Australians.

Origin The expression is American in origin, and it was coined in the mid-19th century, during the time of the California gold rush. Miners panning for gold would put sand and gravel from the river bed into the pan and keep shaking it till everything was level: only then were they able to tell if there was ore in it or not.

Lick into shape

Meaning to succeed in making something or someone presentable after considerable effort.

Examples Harini has been given two days to lick the massive report into shape.

Leave it to Bala. I'm sure he'll lick the students into shape in two days' time.

Origin For a very long time, people believed that when bear cubs were born, they were just a hairy ball. They were of the opinion that it was the mother bear's constant licking which resulted in the cubs getting any shape at all! The cubs were literally licked into shape by the mother!

Like a cat on a hot tin roof

Meaning looking very nervous; unable to sit or stand still in one place.

Examples You should have seen Surendran before the interview. He was like a cat on a hot tin roof.

What's wrong with Hema? She is like a cat on a hot tin roof today.

Origin A cat on a hot tin roof is likely to be very jumpy: just like a nervous person.

Like pulling teeth

Meaning something that is extremely difficult to do.

Examples Getting information from people who work in government offices is like pulling teeth.

Trying to get my grandmother to talk about her childhood was like pulling teeth.

Origin Pulling a tooth out of a person/animal is very difficult.

Lily-livered

Meaning a weakling/coward; someone who can be easily pushed around. Other expressions that have the same meaning are 'white-livered' and 'pigeon-livered'.

Examples The lily-livered Head of Department refused to take action against the students.

Unlike Anand, Usha is certainly not lily-livered. Don't underestimate her.

Origin The ancient Greeks and Romans believed that the liver was not only the seat of love, but also the seat of virile passion, like courage. According to them, the liver of a person full of passion would be red or reddish brown in colour. When you accuse someone of being lily-livered, you are suggesting that his liver is like the lily – white or rather pale in colour. It lacks the blood to make it reddish brown. Whenever the Greeks sacrificed an animal before a battle, they always checked its liver. If the liver of the animal was red, then it was seen as a good omen. If, on the other hand, it was pale, it signified defeat.

Line one's pockets

Meaning make money in an illegal manner; to profit at the expense of others.

Examples Many of our politicians are more interested in lining their pockets than in serving the people.

You can't really blame Yuktha for wanting to line her pockets.

Origin Beau Brummel, an English aristocrat, was a fashion icon. His friends and other members of the aristocracy imitated his style of dressing. A man who wished to become Brummel's personal tailor sent him a new coat to try on. To ensure that the fashion icon liked the coat, the tailor lined the pockets with money.

Lion's share

Meaning the larger share of something.

Examples Promod claimed the lion's share of the credit for winning the match.

They were supposed to divide the money equally between themselves, but Sukesh took the lion's share.

Origin The expression owes its origin to a story from *Aesop's Fables*. In the story, a lion and his three friends – a fox, an ass and a wolf – go hunting. After they make a kill, the lion says that he is going to keep three-fourths of the meat for himself. The reasons he provides for keeping the 'lion's share' are the following: a fourth as his just share, a fourth for his lioness and cubs, and the other one-fourth for his courage. The lion then goes on to inform his friends that he is prepared to part with the remaining portion of the kill, provided one of them defeats him in a fight. The three friends refuse to take him on, and leave the entire kill to the king of beasts.

Live high off the hog

Meaning leading a comfortable life; having enough money to enjoy all the good things in life.

Examples Ever since he got the promotion, Shekar has been living high off the hog.

Renu has been living high off the hog ever since she won the lottery.

Origin A hog is a pig, and the best cuts of meat in this animal are located high up on its sides. These choice cuts of meat are pretty expensive. If an individual is able to buy meat from the high end of the hog every day, then it stands to reason that he is leading a very comfortable life.

Live the life of Riley

Meaning leading a very comfortable life; one where a person seldom has to work hard or spend sleepless nights worrying about making ends meet.

Examples While Prabha worked all day, Sunil stayed home living the life of Riley.

The young couple moved into a big house and led the life of Riley.

Origin No one is really sure who this person was. Some scholars argue that Riley (originally spelt 'Reilly') refers to the character that appeared in a song written by Pat Rooney in 1890. In the song, Riley says New York would 'swim in wine, when the White House and Capitol are mine.' Others argue that it was the American poet, James Whitcomb Riley, who gave rise to the idiom. Apparently, Riley (1849–1916) wrote sentimental poems about young boys, lazing around during the summer without a care in the world – wandering about barefoot, swimming in the river and fishing.

Live up to its billing

Meaning to live up to one's expectations; the show was as good as the advertisement claimed it would be.

Examples I saw the film yesterday. Unfortunately, it didn't live up to its billing.

According to most critics, the play lives up to its billing.

Origin In the old days, promoters used posters and leaflets to let the public know that a new play was going to be staged soon. These various forms of advertisements were called 'bills'. When a well-known actor played the lead, his name was written rather prominently; sometimes, it appeared at the top of the poster or leaflet. It is from this practice that we get the expression 'top billing'. When you say that a movie lived up to its billing, you mean it was as good as the 'bill' (advertisement) claimed it would be.

Lock horns with

Meaning to argue or fight with someone in a very determined way

Examples The two parties locked horns over the recent price hike in petrol.

The students decided not to lock horns with the old professor.

Origin In the animal kingdom, males fight with each other in order to mate with a female. When animals with horns (like deer, moose and rams) fight each other, they invariably lock horns. They get entangled and the fighting becomes rather fierce.

Long face

Meaning to look sad.

Examples The Principal has been walking around with a long face.

It was evident from Rita's long face that something was seriously wrong.

Origin When people are sad, the mouth droops and the eyes become downcast, thus giving the impression that the face has grown longer.

Long in the tooth

Meaning someone who is ageing or getting old.

Examples Most of my aunts and uncles are long in the tooth.

I expected the new professor to be long in the tooth. He wasn't.

Origin The 'tooth' referred to is that of a horse. As a horse begins to grow old, its gums slowly begin to recede. The result is that the animal's teeth begin to look long. The older the animal grows, the more the gums recede, and the longer its teeth become. The age of a horse is usually determined by the size of its teeth.

Look like death warmed over

Meaning — to look terribly ill. It is also possible to say 'like death warmed up'.

Examples — I saw Girish at the hospital. He looked like death warmed over.

What's the matter with you? You look like death warmed up.

Origin — The expression was first used to refer to people with a hangover. After a night of heavy drinking, people usually look pale and sick the following morning.

Look like something the cat dragged in

Meaning — to look untidy or dirty.

Examples — After playing in the mud, the children looked like something the cat dragged in

Our Principal always looks like something the cat dragged in.

Origin Cats, though very clean animals themselves, tend to drag in very strange objects: dead rats, mice, birds, etc.

Look the other way

Meaning to deliberately ignore something; choose to look in the wrong direction.

Examples The soldier saw the child steal an apple, but he chose to look the other way.

The businessman told the Income Tax officer that she would be given a lot of money if she chose to look the other way.

Origin The idiom needs no explanation.

Loose cannon

Meaning someone whose actions cannot be controlled or predicted; independent.

Examples Jayanth is a loose cannon. I don't want him on my team.

Rajni, the loose cannon in the Vice Chancellor's office, has been leaking stories to the press.

Origin In the old days, in order to protect themselves from pirates, shipping companies equipped their vessels with heavy cannons. It was the job of the crew to ensure that these heavy guns were secured tightly. If a chained cannon came loose during a storm or battle, it rolled about the deck causing serious damage to the ship.

Lose face

Meaning something that a person said or did that makes those around him stop respecting him; to be publicly humiliated.

Examples The pilots didn't want to call off the strike because they were afraid to lose face.

I don't understand Kavitha at all. She is more afraid of losing face than losing her property.

Origin English has borrowed extensively from other languages: Latin, Greek, etc. The idiom 'lose face' is actually a translation of the Chinese expression 'tiu lien', meaning 'lose face'.

Lost in the shuffle

Meaning a plan or an idea that does not get the attention that it deserves. The expression can be used with people as well.

Examples In refugee camps, orphans often get lost in the shuffle and are left without food for days.

Our team spent a week coming up with plans. Unfortunately, some of the really good ones got lost in the shuffle.

Origin This American expression comes from the world of card games. When you shuffle a pack of cards, you mix them up; you do not know where a particular card is.

Lotus eater

Meaning someone who is devoted to pleasure and luxury; indifferent to one's responsibilities in the real world.

Examples When the markets crashed, John knew that his life as a lotus eater was over.

Jeevan's friends were very rich. Surprisingly, they were all very hard working; not lotus eaters.

Origin The expression comes from Homer's epic, *The Odyssey*. During one of his voyages to North Africa, Odysseus comes across a group of people who are in a state of dreamy forgetfulness. They have forgotten their real-world responsibilities because of the lotus fruit and flower that they eat every day; they spend most of their time daydreaming, instead.

Love me, love my dog

Meaning to like a person for what he is; to accept someone despite all his faults.

Examples When my aunt started cribbing about me, I said, "Love me, love my dog".

I know I'm not much of a looker and I have a lousy temper. But love me, love my dog.

Origin The idiom is a translation of the Latin expression, 'Qui me amat, amet et canem meum'. The famous abbot, St. Bernard, used it more than 900 years ago.

Make a good fist of something

Meaning an old expression used in informal contexts to mean 'to do something well/successfully'.

Examples This was Runa's first series as captain. I think she made a good fist of it.

Anil has a bad temper. He made a poor fist of being a trouble-shooter.

Origin According to some scholars, the word 'fist' in the expression is used in the sense of 'hand' – someone who does physical work. The opposite of this expression is 'to make a poor fist of something' – meaning 'to fail or be unsuccessful in your attempt to do something'.

Make a practice of

Meaning to make a habit of something; to do something frequently.

Examples Seema makes a practice of giving ten percent of her salary to charity.

Some teachers don't mind if their students come late to class. But they don't want them to make a practice of it.

Origin The meaning is fairly obvious.

Make a silk purse out of a sow's ear

Meaning it is impossible to make something fine out of an inferior or substandard material. The idiom is normally used in the negative. It is also possible to say, 'turn a sow's ear into a silk purse'.

Examples No matter how hard you try, I am afraid you will not succeed in helping him get through his Board exams. You cannot make a silk purse out of a sow's ear.

I wouldn't spend too much time and money trying to repair that old car. You can't turn a sow's ear into a silk purse.

Origin A 'sow' is a female pig. It is not possible to make a silk purse out of a pig's ear.

Pronunciation The word 'sow' rhymes with 'how', 'now' and 'cow'.

Make a splash

Meaning to create a sensation; to make waves.

Examples Vikram Seth's book, *The Golden Gate*, made a splash several years ago.

Vijay's daughter is hoping to make a splash with her first movie.

Origin Very often, people jump into a pool and create a big splash just to get noticed.

Make heavy weather of something

Meaning to take too much time to do something that is fairly simple; having difficulty completing a simple task.

Examples The bowling was mediocre, but our batsmen made heavy weather of it.

This is a simple recipe. You should be able to make the dish in twenty minutes. Don't make heavy weather of it.

Origin Sailors used the expression 'heavy weather' to refer to rough sea conditions. When the sea became choppy, it became difficult to do even some of the simplest things.

Make no bones about it

Meaning to speak frankly, honestly; not try to hide the truth.

Examples The teachers made no bones about their dissatisfaction with the contents of the article.

Radha made no bones about her dislike of crossword puzzles.

Origin During the early 14th century, dice were usually made out of bones, and therefore the slang term for these small cubes was 'bones'. Even today, it is common practice among gamblers to talk to their dice and blow kisses on them before rolling them on the table. When a person makes 'no bones about it', he throws the dice without really doing any of these things. In other words, he makes no attempt to coax the dice to give him the number he wants.

Make one's hair stand on end

Meaning to frighten or terrify someone.

Examples The terrible howl from the dog made my hair stand on end.

Some of the scenes in the movie made my hair stand on end.

Origin When animals are suddenly confronted by danger, the hair around their neck area becomes stiff and stands up straight. This happens in the case of humans as well.

Make sheep eyes at

Meaning to make it rather obvious to a person that you are attracted to him/her.

Examples Some of the girls in class have been making sheep eyes at the new teacher.

I'd be careful if I were you. Your best friend is making sheep eyes at your new girlfriend.

Origin The expression is considered rather old fashioned, and no one is really sure of its origin.

Make the fur fly

Meaning to cause trouble by creating a major disturbance; to do things very quickly.

Examples When the Principal sees what we have done, he's sure to make the fur fly.

Nikitha and Sindhu rearranged the room in a matter of minutes. They really made the fur fly.

Origin In the United States, it was common practice among the settlers to capture racoons, tie them up and then turn the dogs on them. In the bloody fight that followed, the poor racoon's fur would fly all over the place. The spectacle of dogs tearing a racoon to bits was considered a sport. In certain contexts, the idiom has the same meaning as 'to make the dust fly' and 'to make the feathers fly'.

Make waves

Meaning to bring about changes that not all people are happy with; to be seen as someone who causes trouble.

Examples This is not the time to make waves. Let's wait a month before going on strike.

Anamika is a good choice. She is diffident and unlikely to make waves.

Origin When the waves become big, the boat rocks; it becomes unsteady.

Man Friday

Meaning faithful and willing attendant, ready to do whatever he is told.

Examples Many believe that Balram is our Chairman's man Friday.

In the novel, Jeeves is Bertram Wooster's man Friday.

Origin In Daniel Defoe's novel, *Robinson Crusoe*, the hero rescues a savage on a Friday and calls him 'Friday'. This person becomes Crusoe's constant companion, and assists him in everything.

Many a slip between the cup and the lip

Meaning do not be overconfident that your plan is sure to succeed because things can go wrong at any time.

Examples Don't be too sure that you will have the project done by tomorrow. Remember, there's many a slip between the cup and the lip.

Angshu kept saying if we win one more match, the World Cup will be ours. What she forgot was there is many a slip between the cup and the lip.

Origin The expression has been around for several centuries. The story goes that Neptune's son, Ancaus, had a beautiful vineyard which he was extremely proud of. He made the many slaves who took care of it work really hard. Once, an overworked slave predicted that his master would not taste the wine produced that year. When the grapes had been plucked and the wine extracted, Ancaus sent for the slave who had made the prediction. He poured out a cup of wine for himself, and asked the slave why his prediction had failed to come true. The slave apparently said, "There's many a slip between the cup and the lip." As Ancaus lifted the cup to taste the new wine, another slave came running and said that a wild boar had entered the vineyard and was destroying everything. Neptune's son put the cup of wine down, and raced to the vineyard. You can probably guess the rest of the story. Ancaus was killed by the boar.

Millstone around one's neck

Meaning a heavy burden or handicap.

Examples The numerous assignments were like a millstone around Radha's neck.

I don't want to run into debt. I certainly don't want that millstone around my neck.

Origin A 'millstone' is a flat circular stone which was used to grind grain. Villagers in India still use it for this purpose. The stones are rather heavy, and anyone carrying one around his neck is carrying a heavy burden indeed!

Mind your p's and q's

Meaning mind your manners; an informal expression asking someone to behave properly and not offend anyone.

Examples If you don't mind your p's and q's, you'll get into trouble.

When you talk to the boss' wife, you had better mind your p's and q's.

Origin One theory is that the 'p' stands for 'please' and the 'q' for 'thank you'. When you talk to others, use these two words as frequently as you can in order to sound polite. The expression is considered to be old fashioned.

Molotov cocktail

Meaning a homemade firebomb.

Examples The men threw several Molotov cocktails into the farmer's house.

The police arrested three men carrying Molotov cocktails.

Origin This so-called 'cocktail' consists of an inflammable liquid in a bottle to which a wick is attached. The wick is then lit and the bottle is thrown at someone or something. The bottle explodes and the object catches fire. 'Molotov cocktail' is named after V. M. Molotov, the man who was the Foreign Minister of the Soviet Union during the Second World War. When Germany invaded Russia, civilians used this cocktail quite successfully to destroy German tanks.

Pronunciation The first and third 'o' in 'Molotov' are pronounced like the 'o' in 'bob', 'mob' and 'sob'. The second 'o' is like the 'a' in 'china' and the 'v' sounds like the 'f' in 'fish', 'fee' and 'fit'. The word is pronounced '**MO**-le-tof', with the stress on the first syllable. In the expression 'Molotov cocktail', the main stress is on the first syllable of 'cocktail'.

Monday morning blues

Meaning feeling of depression one gets on Monday mornings.

Examples Looks like Aditya has the Monday morning blues.

I don't feel like going to work today. I guess it's a case of the Monday morning blues.

My vacation starts today. So, no Monday morning blues for another month.

Origin Not many people like Mondays; most people get up feeling rather depressed on this day. Reason? They know they have to work for another five or six days before they get some time off. As for 'blues', see 'Feeling blue'.

Monkey business

Meaning mischievous or illegal activity of some kind.

Examples The children must be up to some monkey business.

There is monkey business going on between the CEO and the GM.

Origin The expression is self explanatory. The general belief is that monkeys are always up to mischief.

Monkey's allowance

Meaning to get paid a trifling amount for the work done.

Examples My uncle gave me a monkey's allowance for helping him clean his garage.

Sheba was given a monkey's allowance, but she didn't seem to mind at all.

Origin After performing tricks for an audience, how is a poor monkey rewarded for the hard work? The master gives him something to eat: a banana or peanuts!

Month of Sundays

Meaning a very long time.

Examples Ashwin says he hasn't seen his cousin in a month of Sundays.

I haven't had breakfast in my favourite restaurant in a month of Sundays.

Origin Most people nowadays look forward to Sundays. In the past, however, this was not the case because people were not allowed to have too much fun on a Sunday. It was seen as a day of prayer: people were expected to go to church and spend the rest of the day thinking of the Lord. Strict laws were passed to ensure that people did not drink, host parties or play games. For some people, Sundays, unlike other days, seemed very long because they were unable to do half the things they wanted to. So, just imagine having a month of Sundays on your hands!

Moonlighting

Meaning to take up a second job to make ends meet; a night job.

Examples Many people in our country have to moonlight in order to feed their family.

Do you know that Veda is moonlighting as a physics teacher in the evenings?

Origin It was common practice in Ireland to distill illicit whiskey under the cover of darkness. This job, which was done by the light of the moon, was called 'moonlighting'. In the United States, whiskey produced in this manner was called 'moonshine'. With the passage of time, 'moonlighting' began to be used for legal activities as well.

More fun than a barrel of monkeys

Meaning great deal of fun.

Examples Sajida's husband is more fun than a barrel of monkeys.

We had more fun than a barrel of monkeys at the party.

Origin Having a barrel full of monkeys can be a great source of entertainment. If something is more fun than a barrelful of monkeys, then it must be great fun indeed.

More than one way to skin a cat

Meaning there are several different ways of achieving something.

Examples You don't have to shout at him, but you can make it obvious you are disappointed with what he did. There's more than one way to skin a cat.

I'm afraid that is not the solution. You must figure out some other way. You know what they say – there's more than one way to skin a cat.

Origin According to some scholars, the 'cat' referred to in the expression is the 'catfish'. Its skin is said to be very tough; it has to be removed to make the fish edible.

Much of a muchness

Meaning very similar, almost the same.

Examples There's very little to choose between the two teams. They are much of a muchness.

According to my father, rock music these days is all much of a muchness.

Origin The idiom is self explanatory.

Murder someone in cold blood

Meaning to kill someone without displaying any emotion; like a cold-blooded animal. The murder is planned and executed in a ruthless manner.

Examples His wife and her lover murdered Rajesh in cold blood.

The Minister was murdered in cold blood in front of his house.

Origin Some three hundred years ago, people believed that the temperature of our blood was determined by the frame of mind we were in. The common belief was, when an individual became excited or angry, the blood in his body began to boil. When he remained calm, the blood was cool. These beliefs are reflected in everyday expressions like 'hot-blooded' and 'in cold blood'. In the 17th century, the expression 'in hot blood' was used to refer to murders committed in a fit of passion. For some strange reason, it went out of use. Scholars believe that the expression 'in cold blood', which first appeared in print in 1711 in Joseph Addison's *The Spectator*, is a translation of the French 'sang-froid'.

Naked truth

Meaning plain truth; unvarnished.

Examples According to Augustine, what he had told the police was the naked truth.

If you go to Bala, don't expect any sugar coating: the naked truth is what you are going to get.

Origin According to an ancient fable, Truth and Falsehood went to have a bath in a river. Falsehood came out first, and put on Truth's clothes. When Truth came out and found her clothes missing, she walked away, saying she would rather go naked than wear Falsehood's clothes.

Neck and crop

Meaning an expression which is frequently used by our cricket commentators to mean 'quickly and comprehensively'. It is rather old fashioned and seldom used by native speakers of English.

Example Teja was on 99 when he was bowled neck and crop.

Origin Though there are many theories, nobody is really sure about the origin of this expression. Some believe it comes from the world of horse riding. When a horse suddenly stops without any warning, the rider is sent flying headlong over the animal's head. The word 'crop' in the expression refers to the horse's 'throat'. The poor rider goes over the horse's head and throat. Others believe that it is not the rider, but the horse that falls. They argue that the original expression was 'neck and croup'; the word 'croup' referring to the backside of the horse. When a horse falls 'neck and crop', both its neck and backside hit the ground.

Neck and neck

Meaning a very close race or contest between two participants; difficult to predict the winner.

Examples Felix and Sudhesh were neck and neck in the spelling competition.

At the two-mile mark, Geetha and Prithi were running neck and neck.

Origin The expression comes from the world of horse racing. Two horses running side by side as they approach the finish line are said to be running 'neck and neck'. In such circumstances, it is difficult to predict the outcome of the event; either animal could win the race. Remember, it is 'neck and neck' and not 'neck to neck'.

Nine days' wonder

Meaning something that arouses interest in people for a short time.

Examples The murder of the professor was a nine days' wonder. Nobody talks about it anymore.

Don't worry. People will forget all about the scandal. It'll be another nine days' wonder.

Origin There are many stories to account for this expression. According to some sources, puppies are born blind; their eyes open after about nine days. During this period, the poor animals hear strange noises, smell different scents, etc. In their blind state, the world remains a mystery. Once their eyes open, however, the strangeness of the world disappears. They get used to their surroundings.

Nip and tuck

Meaning mostly limited to American English and has more or less the same meaning as 'neck and neck'. When you say that a game is 'nip and tuck', what you are suggesting is that the two teams are evenly matched. It will therefore be difficult to predict which team will win; the game is too close to call.

Examples It's difficult to say which political party will win. It's nip and tuck right now.

It was nip and tuck till the fifteenth over. After that, Maxwell exploded.

Origin No one is really sure about the origin of the expression. Some people believe that the original expression was 'rip and tuck'. Nowadays, 'nip and tuck' is mostly used to refer to some form of plastic surgery.

Nitpicking

Meaning to examine someone's work very minutely and find fault with it; to focus on the unimportant details.

Examples When I submitted the report, the boss indulged in a lot of petty nitpicking.

At the meeting, the Chairman did not allow any nitpicking criticism.

Origin Remember the days when you went to school and came home with lice in your hair? When you complained to your mother, she immediately brought out her special comb, ran it through your hair for an hour or so and picked off the lice, one by one. What your mother was doing was 'nitpicking'. 'Nit' refers to the egg of a louse or any other parasitic insect. As everyone knows, getting rid of the unwanted nits is a very demanding task; one has to examine the head of the individual very minutely.

No love lost between them

Meaning the two people/parties do not like each other. There is bad blood between them, and they make no effort to hide their contempt for each other.

Examples Right now, there's no love lost between the captains of the two teams.

You can tell by the way she is talking to him that there is no love lost between them.

Origin It is self explanatory.

Nook and cranny

Meaning every part of some place; remote corners and cracks.

Examples The children looked for the ball in every nook and cranny, but they couldn't find it.

I've worked in this school for over twenty years. I know every nook and cranny of it.

Origin Since the 14th century, the word 'nook' (rhymes with 'book' and 'cook') has been used to refer to a remote corner or secluded spot. The word 'cranny', which rhymes with 'granny' and 'nanny', means a crack or an opening of some kind – for example, a crack in the wall can be referred to as 'cranny'.

Nose in the air

Meaning to be very proud, conceited.

Examples Ever since Vikram got his promotion, he's had his nose in the air.

Why would I ask Deepa to go out with me? Her nose is always in the air.

Origin People who are proud never look at those around them; they walk with their head tilted up. They walk with their nose in the air, and when they do look at someone, they look at the individual down their nose.

Not care a hoot

Meaning — an informal expression meaning 'to be completely indifferent to someone or something'; not care at all about what the person has said or about the thing that has happened.

Examples — Divya doesn't care a hoot about what Ganesh thinks of her paintings.

I don't care a hoot if India loses all its matches.

Origin — According to some scholars, the 'hoot' in the expression does not refer to an owl's cry. They believe that 'hoot' was a slang term used to refer to the smallest or tiniest bit of something. Therefore, when you say, 'I don't care a hoot', you mean that you don't care one bit.

Not enough room to swing a cat

Meaning — small; not enough room or space.

Examples — The bedrooms are very small. There's not enough room to swing a cat.

The advertisement said that the rooms were large. When I went there, I found there wasn't enough room to swing a cat.

Origin According to some scholars, the 'cat' refers to a whip used by the captain of a ship. The whip was called 'cat-o'-nine-tails', and in everyday speech, it was invariably reduced to 'cat'. If you want to hit somebody really hard with a whip, you need to take a big swing. If the place you are in is small, then it does not allow you to take such a swing: you do not have the room required to swing the cat.

Not to put too fine a point on it

Meaning a polite way of saying, 'Excuse me for being blunt, but this is what I think'. The expression is normally used when you wish to speak your mind, and are not unduly worried about how the others around you will react.

Examples Your dissertation, Srinivas, not to put too fine a point on it, should be thrown into the dustbin.

Our college team's performance, not to put too fine a point on it, was terrible.

Nuts and bolts

Meaning to know the basics of something; to have practical rather than theoretical knowledge about something.

Examples They tell me that Mohan is familiar with the nuts and bolts of television scripting.

Once you learn the nuts and bolts of making a presentation, you won't be scared anymore.

Origin Nuts and bolts are the basic components of all machines.

Off the cuff

Meaning spontaneous, without any preparation.

Examples Please give Ramdas time to prepare. His off the cuff speeches are terrible.

Stick to the script given. Don't make any off the cuff remarks, please.

Origin Sometimes, a person is called upon to make a speech without any prior intimation. On such occasions, in the old days, the speaker jotted down whatever points he could think of on the cuffs of his shirt. When he stood up to speak, he read the points off the cuff, and elaborated on them.

Old chestnut

Meaning a story or joke that is so old that it is no longer funny. Informal expression used to show disapproval.

Examples Please, we don't want to listen to that old chestnut again.

The speech given by our Vice Chancellor was full of old chestnuts.

Origin The expression comes from a play written by William Diamond. In it, a character keeps telling a joke about a cork tree repeatedly. On one occasion, another character who is sick of hearing the joke, stops him by saying that the tree in question was a chestnut and not a cork tree: "A chestnut. I've heard you tell the joke 27 times, and I'm sure it was a chestnut."

On the back burner

Meaning to postpone doing something; to not act on something because it does not require one's immediate attention.

Examples My cousins are coming over next weekend. So, my plans of going to Kodaikanal with my friends have been put on the back burner.

Because the students have been on strike, teachers have been compelled to put the unit tests and the assignments they give at this time of the month on the back burner.

Origin A big stove usually has two burners in the front and two in the back. Items that do not require the cook's immediate attention are usually put on the back burner.

On the wagon

Meaning informal expression used to refer to someone who has given up drinking alcohol; a heavy drinker attempting to kick the habit. The opposite is 'off the wagon'. In this case, an individual who had stopped drinking, takes to the bottle again.

Examples Abhay is a changed man. He's been on the wagon for six months now.

Girish is trying really hard to stay on the wagon.

Origin The original form of this expression was 'on the water wagon' or 'on the water cart'. The wagon/cart in the idiom was not used to distribute water among people; it was, in fact, employed to keep the streets clean. During the 1890s, there was a concerted effort by many in the United States to bring about Prohibition. Men who vowed to stop drinking would often get onto the water wagons and take an oath that when they became thirsty, they would quench their thirst by drinking a couple of glasses of water from the wagon

Once bitten twice shy

Meaning having had a bad experience previously, there is a reluctance to put oneself in the same situation again.

Examples The caterers arrived three hours late last time, so Rama is not hiring them again. I guess it's a case of once bitten twice shy.

The last time he ate fish, Pradeep almost choked. He's stopped eating fish altogether – once bitten twice shy.

Origin If you have been bitten by a dog, you are going to be wary of dogs all your life.

Once in a blue moon

Meaning something that happens rarely.

Examples My brother Paul lives in Russia. I see him once in a blue moon.

How often does Tendulkar come to office? Once in a blue moon.

Origin There are several explanations for the origin of this expression. According to scientists, whenever a volcano erupts, the sulphur and dust particles that are thrown up into the atmosphere often cause the moon to appear blue for some time. When the volcano on Krakatoa (an island between Java and Sumatra) exploded in 1883, rocks were hurled thirty miles high into the air and dust from the volcano fell nearly three thousand miles away. After this eruption, the moon looked blue for several days.

Another explanation offered by scholars is the following. On very rare occasions, we have two full moons within the same month. The editors of *Maine Farmer's Almanac* used to indicate the first full moon of the month in red and the second, when it did occur, in blue!

One swallow does not make a summer

Meaning an expression used to caution people; one good omen does not necessarily mean a happy ending. Advising someone to err on the side of caution.

Examples As soon as we launched the product, we got a huge order from Russia. We were all pretty excited. But our boss reminded us that one swallow does not make a summer.

The first experiment is a huge success, but we should remember that one swallow does not make a summer.

Origin — This is another expression which became popular thanks to *Aesop's Fables*. In the story, a young man sees a swallow on a relatively warm winter day. Since swallows are seen only during spring, the young man thinks that spring has arrived. As a result, he sells his winter coat and then proceeds to drink with the money he has made. A few days later, the weather turns extremely cold again, and the young man shivering in the cold realises that one swallow does not necessarily imply that spring has arrived. Other expressions which have more or less the same meaning are 'one grain does not fill a sack' and 'one actor cannot make a play'.

One-trick pony

Meaning — a person who is good at one thing; someone who has tasted success once.

Examples — After a string of flops, Kumar has been labelled a one-trick pony.

You can't ask Hemant to help you with the accounts. He is a one-trick pony.

Origin — This person is like the pony in a circus which is capable of doing one trick, and one trick alone.

Open a can of worms

Meaning: to intentionally or unintentionally create problems for yourself or for someone else; to make a situation worse.

Examples: The statement by the Minister has opened up a can of worms.

Please don't even mention his sister. If you do, you'll be opening a can of worms.

Origin: In the U.S., it was common practice for stores near the lakeside to make fresh bait available for those interested in fishing. Earthworms were dug up, put in cans, and sold. When the fisherman opened the can, some of the wriggling worms fell out. Picking the slimy things up and putting them back in the container was not an easy thing to do. By opening the can of worms, the fisherman had created problems for himself.

Out of kilter

Meaning: a machine that is malfunctioning; not in proper working order. An opinion that is very different from those of others.

Examples: Our TV has been out of kilter for the past two weeks.

Mom, the TV is out of kilter again!

The President's views were out of kilter with public opinion.

Origin — The word 'kilter' comes from the English 'kelter', meaning 'in good condition'; something that is 'out of kilter' is no longer in working order – it is malfunctioning.

Out of my hair

Meaning — to feel extremely relieved because the source of annoyance is gone.

Examples I have been with these two brats the whole day. Could you take them to the park just to get them out of my hair?

Who cares where Yadav went? He's out of my hair, and that's what really matters.

Origin When a person has something stuck in his hair, he feels extremely annoyed or irritated when he is unable to remove it.

Out of sorts

Meaning to be slightly ill or unwell; not be one's usual self. Can also be used to mean 'irritable'.

Examples Is something wrong, Madhu? You look out of sorts today.

Shruthi always feels out of sorts on Monday mornings.

Origin According to some scholars, the expression comes from the world of printing. In the past, typesetters composed each page manually; it was a laborious process. The person first picked the letters that made up a word and then put them together. In the world of printing, these letters were called 'sorts'. Sometimes, while composing a page, the typesetter ran out of sorts. When this happened, he often became irritated or frustrated.

Paddle one's own canoe

Meaning — to be self reliant or independent; charting one's own course.

Examples — Listen, Naresh, you are 25 years old. It's time you started to paddle your own canoe.

I don't think Anamika is interested in paddling her own canoe.

Origin — A 'canoe' is a small boat which Native Americans used. If you had the ability to paddle your own canoe, you could go anywhere you wanted to. You were not dependent on anyone.

Isn't she too young to start paddling her own canoe?

Pronunciation The 'a' in canoe is like the 'a' in 'china', and the final 'oe' is like the 'oo' in 'cool', 'pool' and 'fool'. The word is pronounced 'ke-**NOO**', with the stress on the second syllable.

Paint the town red

Meaning to celebrate wildly, especially during the night.

Examples When Ranjit heard that he had got the contract, he and his friends painted the town red.

I need to get some rest. I have been painting the town red the past two nights.

Origin Many theories have been put forward to explain the origin of this expression. Some people believe that in the old days when an army captured a town, soldiers smeared the blood of their fallen opponents on the doors of houses. They went about literally painting the town red. According to another theory, when a person drinks too much, his nose and face turn red.

Pandora's box

Meaning a source of complication, something that will create many new and unexpected problems. The common expression is 'open a Pandora's box'.

Examples The Finance Minister's reforms opened a Pandora's box of industrial problems.

The Vice Chancellor refused to discuss the matter as he didn't want to open a Pandora's box.

Origin The expression has its origins in Greek mythology. Zeus, the King of Gods, was fed up with mankind, and in order to teach them a lesson, he created a woman – Pandora. The King of Gods then asked all the other gods to shower gifts on her; gifts which would ultimately bring about the downfall of mankind! The gifts were put in a beautiful box, and Zeus presented it to Pandora, warning her never to open it. Like most curious people, she opened it and saw to her horror all the evils of this world escape. According to some scholars, it was not Pandora who opened the box, but her husband, Epimetheus. As for the name 'Pandora', 'pan' in Greek means 'all' and 'dora' means 'gifts'.

Paper tiger

Meaning something or someone who looks formidable, but in fact, is weak and ineffectual.

Examples My boss is nothing more than a paper tiger.

The new set of rules is idiotic. It has reduced people in top positions to paper tigers.

Origin — The expression comes from a Chinese proverb. It was made famous in English by Chairman Mao Tse Tung, the leader of the Communist Party of China, when he claimed that the United States was nothing more than a paper tiger. Later, during the Korean War, he called the then U.S. President, Truman, the same thing.

Par for the course

Meaning — what is happening is normal and acceptable for the given situation.

Examples — Many companies in our country are planning to downsize. But then, that's par for the course.

The Government is planning to increase its budget for education. That's par for the course.

Origin — The expression comes from the world of golf. When you play a round of golf, you are allowed 72 strokes to sink the ball into the 18 holes. If you do it in 72 strokes, you are par for the course. If you complete the round in less than 72 strokes, then you are said to be 'under par'.

Pass the buck

Meaning — putting the blame for something that has gone wrong on someone else; find a scapegoat, and pin the blame on him.

Examples For a change, our Director didn't pass the buck. He admitted that what he had done was wrong.

Don't try to pass the buck, Anu. It's your fault we missed the train.

Origin Scholars are of the opinion that the word 'buck' is the short form of either 'buckshot' (a bullet) or 'buckhorn knife'. The knife was so called because its handle was made from a buck's (a male deer) horn. When poker was played, one of these items was placed in front of the person who functioned both as the dealer and the 'bank'. Whenever the dealer changed, the buck was placed in front of the new dealer. The buck was literally passed from one dealer to another!

Pay through one's nose

Meaning to pay a heavy price for something; to pay too much for it.

Examples Maya liked the painting so much she was willing to pay through her nose for it.

Never go to that restaurant. You have to pay through your nose for most things.

Origin According to some scholars, this expression came into use between the 9th and 10th centuries when the Vikings ruled over much of Ireland. The rulers apparently levied a 'nose tax' on the Irish. The people who failed to pay the tax were punished by having their nose slit! The poor Irish were forced to pay a lot of money just to keep their nose intact!

Peeping Tom

Meaning — a man who watches women secretly, and becomes aroused when they begin to undress.

Examples — The police caught a peeping Tom just outside the women's hostel.

I saw a peeping Tom trying to look through Suchitra's window.

Origin — The story goes that Leofric III, Lord of Coventry, imposed heavy taxes on his poor tenants. When his wife, Lady Godiva, pleaded with him to be more sympathetic, Leofric told her he would lower the taxes, provided she rode through the town of Coventry naked. In order to help the people, Lady Godiva decided to do the unthinkable. She informed the people of Coventry why she would be riding through the town naked, and requested them to keep their doors and windows closed as she passed through each street. She asked them not to peep. On the appointed day, most of the people of Coventry respected her wishes and stayed indoors, with the doors and windows firmly shut. The only exception was the tailor, Tom. He peeped through the window and saw the naked figure of Lady Godiva. According to one version of the story, peeping Tom was struck blind as soon as he saw her.

Pencil in

Meaning a temporary appointment, something that can be changed.

Examples The dentist said he would pencil me in for next Thursday.

Could you please pencil me in for tomorrow?

Origin When we write with a pencil, we know it is something that can be erased; it is not permanent.

Pete's sake

Meaning the expression is mostly used in speech to indicate surprise, anger or disgust. It has the same meaning as 'for heaven's sake', 'for goodness' sake', 'for God's sake', 'for pity's sake', etc.

Examples For Pete's sake, don't just stand there like an idiot. Give me a hand.

Drive a little more slowly, for Pete's sake. You almost hit an old woman.

Origin The 'Pete' refers to St. Peter. Nowadays, it is very common to hear people swear when they are angry or exasperated. In the old days, people were not allowed to take the Lord's name in vain; they were punished if they did so. In order to avoid swearing, people began to make use of euphemisms – mild and less harsh sounding expressions – 'for Pete's sake' was one such euphemism.

Pie in the sky

Meaning something that will never be realised. A reward that you are hoping to get in the future; chances are, it will not happen.

Examples My boss has promised me a big raise next year, but I think it's just pie in the sky.

Jai's ideas about reforming the tax system are nothing more than pie in the sky.

Origin It is believed that the expression was made popular in the U.S. by the radical labour union organiser, Joe Hill. Here are some lines from his song, *The Preacher and the Slave*: "Work and pray/Live on hay/You'll get pie in the sky when you die!"

Pillar to post

Meaning forced to move from one place to another; wasting a lot of energy running around and achieving nothing.

Examples The old man was made to run from pillar to post for his son's death certificate.

Rima has contacts. She'll make sure you won't have to run from pillar to post.

Origin In the past, prisoners who had been found guilty, were often taken to the market place, tied to a 'post' and then whipped. The bleeding prisoner was then dragged to a pillory – a wooden frame with three holes in it. The prisoner's head and his two hands were put through each hole, and the poor man was forced to remain in this awkward position for several days together. The members of the public often entertained themselves by throwing eggs and rotten vegetables at him. According to scholars, the original expression was 'to run from post to pillar'.

Pin money

Meaning mostly used nowadays to refer to a very small sum of money that a person earns or is given so that he can spend it on things he wants, but does not necessarily need. In the past, it referred to the small allowance that a husband gave his wife to buy things for herself.

Examples Teaching children English in the evenings gave Usha some pin money.

I did a little bit of shopping with the pin money I had.

Origin When the ordinary pin was introduced in England, it was very expensive and always in short supply. Pins were sold only on one or two days in a year. The original 'pin money' was the regular allowance that a husband gave his wife so that she could buy pins when they became available. With the passage of time, pins became plentiful, and the term 'pin money' began to be used to refer to a small amount of money that one spent on oneself.

Pink of health

Meaning to be in excellent health.

Examples I'm doing fine. I'm in the pink of health.

The 80-year-old man was in the pink of health.

Origin According to some scholars, the expression has nothing to do with the colour. 'Pink' is the name used to refer to the flower, 'dianthus'. It is considered by many to be the perfect flower. Hence, when you say you are in the pink, what you mean is that you are in perfect health. Others believe that 'pink' refers to the scarlet-coloured jackets that people wore when they went fox hunting. Therefore, when you say that you are in the pink, it means that you are in good health, ready to go hunting. Another theory is connected with the complexion of Caucasians. Being fair in complexion, when they are in good health, their cheeks are pink.

Pink slip

Meaning: letter informing an employee that his services are no longer required. It can be used as a verb as well.

Examples: More than twenty workers were given the pink slip today.

My boss says that I'll be getting the pink slip next month.

If Hari's performance doesn't improve, I'll have to pink slip him.

They pink slipped nearly two hundred people yesterday.

Origin: The story goes that in the late 1800s, workers sometimes received, along with their pay cheque, a letter written on pink stationery. The letter usually informed the receiver that his services were no longer required. This letter written on pink paper began to be called 'pink slip'. In Germany, when a person gets fired, he does not get 'the pink slip', but 'the blue letter'. The French, on the other hand, refer to such a letter as 'yellow paper'.

Pipe dream

Meaning a fantasy; a wish or desire that is unlikely to come true.

Examples Wanting to buy a house in this neighbourhood is nothing more than a pipe dream.

Getting Indians to follow traffic rules! That's a pipe dream.

Origin According to scholars, the pipe refers to the one used by drug addicts to smoke opium. When someone smokes opium, he hallucinates.

Plain sailing

Meaning used in informal contexts to mean 'smooth and easy progress'. Something that is 'plain sailing', goes off without a hitch or problem. 'Clear sailing' and 'smooth sailing' mean the same thing.

Examples Your first few months on the job will not be plain sailing.

We left at 3:00 AM. So, the drive to the village was plain sailing.

Origin In the past, when sailors calculated the distance between two points, they did so based on the assumption that the earth was flat and not spherical. To simplify calculations, sailors assumed that the ship was sailing on a flat or a 'plane surface'. The original expression was, in fact, 'plane sailing'. As spelling had not been standardised, the two words 'plain' and 'plane' were used interchangeably. When the expression made its first appearance in print in the 17th century, the word was spelt 'plain' instead of 'plane' – and everyone followed suit. The idiom acquired its figurative meaning – slow and easy progress – over a period of time.

Play into someone's hands

Meaning to unintentionally do what your opponent wants you to.

Examples By sneaking the information to her colleagues, Maya played right into the Principal's hands.

Don't react whenever Kishore teases you. If you do, you'll be playing into his hands.

Origin When you play bridge, you attempt to get the opponent to play certain cards. When you compel him to discard cards he does not want to, you are forcing him to 'play into your hands'.

Play it by ear

Meaning to improvise; to respond to a situation intuitively, without thinking too far ahead.

Examples I have no clue how Nalini's parents are going to react. I'll have to play it by ear.

Mukund doesn't know how much time he'll be spending with his ailing aunt. He said that he would play it by ear.

Origin This expression, which is mostly used in informal contexts, comes from the world of music. When a musician 'plays it by ear', he attempts to play or reproduce a piece of music without looking at the music sheet. He plays the piece from memory, and uses his ears to determine if what he is playing is correct or not.

Play possum

Meaning to pretend to be asleep or dead.

Examples When he saw the bear, the hunter lay down on the ground and played possum.

I don't think Renu wants to help us with the cleaning. She's in bed playing possum.

Origin A 'possum' is a small furry animal which when threatened, pretends to be dead. It goes into a coma-like state: the body becomes stiff, and a foul smell emanates from it. Even when its attacker rolls it around and prods it, it shows no signs of life. Thinking that the animal is dead, thc would-be attacker moves on. The possum emerges from its coma-like state sometime later, and goes about its business.

Play second fiddle

Meaning to take a back seat to someone; to be in a subordinate position. The idiom can also be used to mean 'second rate' or 'second best'.

Examples I'm sure Gopal is sick and tired of playing second fiddle to Thara.

Deepshika is not the sort of person who will play second fiddle to anyone.

Origin The 'fiddle' refers to the violin. In an orchestra, violinists and other musicians are often categorised into classes: first, second, third, etc. The first violinist plays a dominant role in the orchestra. The second fiddle or violin ends up taking a back seat.

Playing both ends against the middle

Meaning to manipulate; to do or say something which causes two individuals or parties to quarrel and use it to your advantage.

Examples Atul is the consummate politician. He will tell you one thing and the exact opposite to someone else. He plays both ends against the middle.

If Anand continues to play both ends against the middle the way he has been, he is not going to have any friends left.

Origin — Refers to a technique used by crooked card dealers when they played the game of faro.

Playing to the gallery

Meaning — someone who instead of doing the job assigned to him, spends his time trying to gain the admiration and support of those around him. Instead of taking tough decisions, he does and says things which will make him popular. Mostly used to show disapproval.

Examples — Most news channels are playing to the gallery.

We need to hire someone who doesn't play to the gallery.

Origin — In the world of theatre, the word 'gallery' referred to the people who sat in the cheapest seats. Any actor or playwright who tried to please the poor and unsophisticated people sitting in these seats was seen to be doing something demeaning – by trying to win their approval, he was doing something inappropriate.

Pleased as Punch

Meaning — to be elated or extremely happy.

Examples Devidas was pleased as Punch when he got his promotion.

The CEO was pleased as Punch when he was told that profits had increased by 25%.

Origin The 'Punch' in the idiom has nothing to do with the drink or the blow that villains receive from our film heroes. It refers to a character in a 17th century puppet show called *Punch and Judy*. The main character, Punch, was a very content person who sang cheerfully all the time.

Plough a lonely/lone furrow

Meaning someone who does things on his own; to do things that others are unwilling to.

Examples Leave Bhalla out. He prefers to plough a lone furrow.

The other members refused to help. Ankita ended up ploughing a lonely furrow.

Origin In order to plant seeds, a farmer makes use of a plough to dig up his field. The deep line that the plough makes as it is dragged is called a 'furrow'.

Pronunciation 'Plough' rhymes with 'cow' and 'how'. The 'u' in 'furrow' sounds like the 'u' in 'cut' and 'but', and the second syllable sounds like the word 'row'. The word is pronounced '**FU**-row', with the stress on the first syllable.

Plume oneself on something

Meaning — to be extremely proud of something that you have achieved/done; to pat yourself on the back.

Examples — The rising star plumed herself on her brilliant performance.

Every now and then, Yogesh plumes himself on his good looks.

Origin — The long feathers that a bird has are referred to as 'plumes'. In order to look their best and attract members of the opposite sex, birds often clean their plumes using their beak. In the past, it was common practice among soldiers to wear such plumes on their helmet: very often, the feather one wore indicated one's rank.

Pound of flesh

Meaning — to take what one is legally entitled to in a ruthless manner; to take what is due to you knowing fully well that by doing so, you are going to create problems for the other person. Usually used to show disapproval. One can 'get/take/demand one's pound of flesh'.

Examples — The family's distress had absolutely no effect on the greedy moneylender. He was determined to get his pound of flesh.

As expected, the three coalition parties are demanding their pound of flesh. What the PM will do is anybody's guess.

Origin It comes from Shakespeare's *Merchant of Venice*. In it, Shylock lends Antonio money on the understanding that should Antonio default on the loan, he would cut off a pound of flesh from his body and give it to Shylock. When Antonio is unable to pay, Shylock demands his pound of flesh.

Preach to the choir/converted

Meaning an American expression used to talk about an attempt to sell others something that they already have. You attempt to sell an idea to someone who already believes in it; you waste your time trying to convince an audience that is already convinced. The expressions 'preach to the choir' and 'preach to the converted' have the same meaning.

Examples Please don't lecture me about the need to keep our streets clean. You are preaching to the choir.

There's no point in talking about family planning to the highly educated. You're merely preaching to the converted.

Origin The choir referred to in the expression is the group of singers you find in a church. If the priest were to talk about the importance of religion to the members of the choir, he would be wasting his time. He would be talking to a group of people who already believe in its importance – otherwise, they would not be in church singing the glory of the Lord.

Pretty penny

Meaning mostly used in informal contexts in American English to mean 'a considerable amount of money'. Something that costs a pretty penny is expensive.

Examples That new car of his must have cost Amit a pretty penny.

The house we looked at costs a pretty penny. I don't think we can afford it.

Origin 'Pretty' in this context has nothing to do with looks; it means 'considerable'. A 'penny' is a one cent coin, and in the expression, it is used to represent money. So, when you say 'pretty penny', you mean 'considerable money'. The expression 'cost a pretty penny' was first used in 1768, and at that time, you could buy a lot of things with a penny.

Proof of the pudding is in the eating

Meaning in order to determine the value of something, one needs to test or try it; do not pass judgement without examining the facts or evidence. The expression is often reduced to 'the proof of the pudding', and it has the same meaning as 'don't judge a book by its cover'.

Examples On paper, your suggestions look great. But you know what they say, the proof of the pudding is in the eating.

I've read the Finance Minister's report. It looks promising, but the proof of the pudding is in the eating.

Pull out all the stops

Meaning to do everything possible to make something a success.

Examples The local police pulled out all the stops to find the terrorists.

The young couple pulled out all the stops for their children's education.

Origin The pipe organ, an instrument that is usually played in church, has small knobs which are referred to as stops. These stops control the amount of air flowing through the pipes of the organ. When a stop is pulled out, the volume increases. The more stops you pull out, the louder the organ sounds.

Pull someone's chestnuts out of the fire

Meaning to do someone else's dirty work for them; the individual is in such a tight spot that you feel compelled to help him, often putting yourself in danger.

Examples As expected, Druv's rich parents pulled chestnuts out of the fire for him once again.

I'm sorry, but I'm not going to help you. I'm sick and tired of pulling your chestnuts out of the fire.

Origin The expression has its origins in a fable. In the story, a cat and a monkey are sitting around a fire, watching their master roast chestnuts. The monkey wants to eat the nuts, but he does not want to pull them out of the fire because doing so would burn his hands. While the master is away, the cunning monkey convinces the poor cat to do his dirty work for him. The cat scoops out the nuts one by one and, in the process, burns his paw. The selfish monkey eats all the nuts, leaving nothing for the foolish cat.

Pull someone's leg

Meaning mostly used nowadays to mean 'to tease or play a joke on someone'. It is always 'leg' and never 'legs'.

Examples I enjoy pulling Devi's leg once in a while.

Sheba was pulling my leg when she said she saw Salman at the airport.

Origin In the old days, it was common practice among robbers to make use of a wire or a cane to trip unsuspecting passers-by. While the stunned victim was on the ground, the other members of the gang relieved him of his valuables.

Pull the wool over someone's eyes

Meaning used in informal contexts to mean 'to deceive someone'.

Examples Raju pulled the wool over the old couple's eyes, and ran away with their savings.

Before buying a car, please read this article. Otherwise, the salesperson will try to pull the wool over your eyes.

Origin Several centuries ago, it was standard practice in Europe and America for men and women to wear wigs – irrespective of whether they were bald or not. These loosely fitting hair pieces were usually made of wool. When thieves wanted to steal something that a wig wearer was carrying, they sneaked up to the individual and literally pulled the wig (wool) over the victim's eyes. Temporarily blinded and confused, the victim was unaware of what was happening around him. The thief used this opportunity to run away with what the victim was carrying.

Pull up one's socks

Meaning — asking someone to put greater effort into what he is doing. You want him to shape up and do a better job because you are rather unhappy with what he has done so far. The expression is mostly limited to British English.

Examples — If you want to work with Madhu, you'd better pull your socks up.

Ganesh needs to pull up his socks if he wants to be the captain of the team.

Origin — According to some scholars, the expression refers to the pre-race ritual that many athletes go through before they take up their position. They do some deep breathing, stretch their arms and legs, and...you've guessed it...pull up their socks.

Purple patch

Meaning — a very successful or a lucky period. The expression 'hit/struck a purple patch' is usually used in sports.

Examples — Your team struck a purple patch at the right time.

Now that Djokovic has hit a purple patch, people expect him to achieve the Golden Slam.

Origin — No one is sure about the exact origin of this expression. Some believe that it is based on the fact that during Roman times, highly successful individuals – like noblemen – wore purple-coloured togas.

Push comes to shove

Meaning — to delay committing oneself to a course of action; to be compelled to take a decision about a matter. People normally say, 'if push comes to shove' or 'when push comes to shove'.

Examples — If push comes to shove, we can always postpone the wedding.

When push came to shove, Mr. Mehta compromised and took a pay cut.

Origin — According to some scholars, the expression comes from the world of rugby.

Put a sock in it

Meaning — Used in informal contexts to mean 'to stop talking or shut up'. Americans say 'put a cork in it'.

Examples Vishnu has gone on long enough. It's about time he put a sock/cork in it.

Put a sock/cork in it, you two. The baby is sleeping.

Origin The first gramophone (record player) had a huge horn fitted on it to serve as a speaker. The gramophone itself did not have a volume control. In order to lower the volume, people used to stuff a sock into the horn!

Put out to pasture/grass

Meaning to retire a person/thing; to compel someone to quit his job.

Examples The Manager will be put out to pasture/grass next year.

Thirty people will be put out to pasture/grass by the end of this month.

Origin In the past, when farm animals like cows, bulls and horses had outlived their usefulness – when they had become too old to work – they were allowed to walk around and graze on their own. No one really took care of these animals

Put up your dukes

Meaning to put up your fists and get ready to fight.

Examples Come on, Chethan, be a man! Put up your dukes.

I'm going to count to three. You'd better put your dukes up by then.

Origin The Duke of Wellington, the man who defeated Napoleon Bonaparte in the Battle of Waterloo in 1815, had a rather prominent nose. The men who served under Wellington began to affectionately refer to any nose which was unusually long as 'duke'. With the pasage of time, the word began to be used to refer to any nose. Since human fists were frequently employed in fights to put a 'duke' out of joint, fists began to be called 'duke busters'. Soon, the word 'busters' was dropped, and everyone started referring to fists as 'dukes'.

Put your foot in your mouth

Meaning to say or do something that is embarrassing.

Examples Whenever he talks to girls, Rahul ends up putting his foot in his mouth.

Hari put his foot in his mouth when he told his pregnant wife to lose some weight.

Put your money where your mouth is

Meaning telling someone to back his words with action; do not just talk, perform.

Examples — If you are serious about helping the street children in our locality, then you should put your money where your mouth is. Donate liberally.

I think you should stop complaining about how corrupt our politicians are. Put your money where your mouth is and contest in the coming elections.

Put your thinking cap on

Meaning — to do some serious thinking; to stop fooling around and give the matter some serious thought.

Examples — Please put your thinking cap on and come up with creative solutions to our problem.

If you wish to get out of the mess you're in, you need to put your thinking cap on.

Origin — The 'cap' in the expression has nothing to do with the kind of caps we wear when playing games. According to some scholars, it refers to the tight-fitting cap that a Judge used to put on before sentencing a criminal. People believed that the cap helped him think!

Pyrrhic victory

Meaning — a victory won at a great cost; paying too high a price for something.

Example It was a pyrrhic victory. By the time Jeet won the case, he was too ill to go anywhere.

Origin King Pyrrhus of Epirus in Greece invaded Italy in 280 BC, and during his campaign against the Romans, he won many battles. After defeating his enemy at Aschulum, Pyrrhus said, "Another such victory and we are undone"; the reason being that he had lost many soldiers in the battle. His army had become so depleted that he was forced to return to Greece without ever setting foot in Rome. Though the King won many battles, he ultimately lost the war! So, when you refer to something as being a 'pyrrhic victory', it implies that you have suffered so many losses that the victory pales into insignificance.

Pronunciation The 'y' in 'pyrrhic' sounds like the 'i' in 'sit', 'hit' and 'bit', and the final syllable sounds like the 'rick' in 'brick', 'rickshaw' and 'cricket'. The stress is on the first syllable. In the expression 'pyrrhic victory', however, the main stress is on the first syllable of 'victory'.

Rain cats and dogs

Meaning to rain heavily; to pour.

Examples It's been raining cats and dogs since last night.

It rained cats and dogs during my sister's wedding.

Origin — In the old days, the street drainage system in Europe was a mess. When there was a heavy downpour, the drains used to get clogged and overflow. Stray dogs and cats used to fall into the drains and drown. When people came out of their houses after the rain had stopped, they found dead animals floating in the drains. It was as if during the heavy downpour, cats and dogs had fallen from the sky!

Raise the bar

Meaning — to set a higher standard; to raise the level of something.

Examples — When the Principal raised the bar, more students ended up failing the exam.

The VC had to lower the bar in order to give the candidate the job.

Origin — The expression comes from the world of athletics. In the track and field event of high jump, when you clear a particular height, the bar is raised to see if you can jump higher. You are being set a new challenge, a higher standard.

Raising Cain

Meaning — to protest angrily about something; to behave in a disruptive manner and create problems for others.

Examples My father raised Cain when he was told that he wasn't entitled to a refund.

When the parents were informed that their children wouldn't be allowed to write the exam, they raised Cain.

Origin Cain and Abel are the sons of Adam and Eve. In a fit of jealousy, Cain kills his younger brother.

Rap on the knuckles

Meaning to speak to someone angrily because he has done something wrong or has failed to do something. The punishment that is given is not very severe; it is usually given to an individual to serve as a warning.

Examples Hema got a sharp rap on the knuckles for not finishing the project on time.

The coach rapped the players on the knuckles for turning up late for practice.

Origin The word 'rap' means 'to hit sharply', and 'knuckles' refer to the joints in one's hands and fingers. Therefore, when you rap someone on his knuckles, what you are doing is hitting the person sharply on the back of his hand. Many teachers in our country rap students on their knuckles even today.

Read the riot act

Meaning: mostly used in British English to mean 'to reprimand someone; to criticise or scold a person quite severely'.

Examples: The teacher read the riot act to the three students who walked in late.

Mother read me the riot act when she caught me smoking.

Origin: In the early decades of the 18th century, the political situation in Britain was rather unstable – people were very angry and unhappy with King George I. To ensure that people did not take matters into their own hands and create chaos, the Riot Act was passed in Parliament in 1714. According to this Act, not more than a dozen people could assemble in public places. If more people came together, then the local law enforcement official ensured the crowd dispersed. He achieved this by reading aloud the Riot Act. If the people chose to ignore the warning, they were put in jail.

Reading between the lines

Meaning: trying to deduce the hidden meaning from what has been said; to figure out the implied or suggested meaning of a speaker.

Examples The Chairman's speech was fine. But, reading between the lines, I figure the company is going to start downsizing soon.

Don't believe whatever the Minister says. Learn to read between the lines.

Origin The expression comes from the world of cryptography, where secret codes are used to write and decipher messages. According to one theory, it was standard practice to write two messages in the same letter. The first message was written with ordinary ink, and the second with invisible ink. The secret message, using invisible ink, was written between the lines written in ordinary ink. Some experts believe that invisible ink was never used. They are of the opinion that if a reader wished to figure out the secret message in the letter, he had to read every other line.

Red faced

Meaning to become very angry or embarrassed about something.

Examples When the teacher's pants tore, he stood red-faced in front of the class.

When the Chairman accused Suman of stealing, she became red-faced.

Origin When people with a fair complexion become angry or embarrassed about something, the blood rushes to their face and makes it look red.

Red herring

Meaning a ploy or distractor; something that is used to turn the focus of attention from something important to something totally insignificant. The expression has a slightly negative connotation.

Examples The killer was never caught because the police were busy chasing red herrings.

Sita found it difficult to solve the mystery. The author had, in her opinion, thrown in too many red herrings.

Origin A 'herring' is a fish that emits a very strong smell. In the past, escaped convicts used this fish to confuse the police dogs tracking them. While he ran, the fugitive dragged a herring along with him. After some time, he threw the fish in one direction while he ran off in the other. The chasing bloodhounds were fooled into following the scent of the herring. The original idiom was 'drag a red herring across the trail'; later, it was shortened to 'red herring'. The colour of the fish is not red, but grey. It turns red when it is 'cured' – i.e., when it is smoked and salted.

Red-letter day

Meaning a very important or a very special day; a day on which something memorable happened or will happen.

Examples The day the school won the championship was a red-letter day for us.

Even after twenty-five years, Vasu considers his wedding day a red-letter day.

Origin The expression comes from the practice that was followed in religious calendars. In the old days, saints' birthdays, festivals and other holy days were marked in red. The other days of the month, which were not special, were marked in black. So, the original 'red-letter day' had a religious significance. It was only during the 18th century that the expression began to take on a general meaning – namely, any memorable or important day in an individual's life.

Red tape

Meaning bureaucratic rules that make it impossible for things to get done quickly.

Examples My leave application has been held up by red tape.

Vijay says he knows how to cut through the red tape.

Origin — The idiom owes its origin to the practice begun by government officials in England in the 17th century. They were in the habit of tying official documents with a ribbon that was red in colour – some people argue that the ribbon was closer to pink than red! The expression 'red tape' was introduced by Charles Dickens and made popular by Thomas Carlyle. By the 19th century, the idiom began to mean 'official sluggishness'. If you have a 'red-tape mind', you apply rules blindly.

Rhyme or reason

Meaning — to do something without really thinking things through; an absence of common sense.

Examples — Meera quit her well-paid job without rhyme or reason.

The customer started shouting at us for no rhyme or reason.

Origin — Sir Thomas More, the author of *Utopia*, is believed to have made this idiom popular. A young writer apparently went to More with a manuscript, and asked him for feedback. After reading it, the Chancellor of Henry VIII suggested that the young man convert it to rhyme. The budding writer did as he was told, and showed it to Sir

Thomas. After reading it, More apparently told the writer, "Now it is somewhat better, for it is rhyme; whereas before, it was neither rhyme nor reason." Not everyone believes this story.

Ride one's hobbyhorse

Meaning to talk about one's favourite topic or subject at length. It is also possible to say 'on one's hobby-horse'.

Examples Don't mention 'corruption'. If you do, Arvind will get started on his hobbyhorse.

Women's empowerment – Janaki has been riding her hobbyhorse all morning.

Origin A 'hobbyhorse' was actually a toy that children played with. It was basically a long stick that had a wooden horse's head attached to it at one end.

Riding roughshod over someone

Meaning to dominate someone quite ruthlessly; to use brute force to obtain the desired results.

Examples The new boss is a bully and rides roughshod over everyone.

The press accused the Opposition of riding roughshod over Parliamentary procedure.

Origin The term 'roughshod' refers to the type of shoe that was often mounted on a horse's hoof. The word 'shod' is related to the word 'shoe'; in order to ensure that the horse did not slip, the shoes were often kept rough. To make sure that the animal had good traction, the blacksmith left the nailheads projecting from the shoes. In times of war, horses were armed with these projecting nails on their hooves; the nails provided better grip on slippery ground and enabled the horse to injure or kill fallen enemy soldiers. It was during the 18th century that the idiom began to mean 'to bully someone'.

Ringside view/seat

Meaning to have an excellent view of an event; to have the best seat in the house.

Examples Sheel was sitting on the terrace and had a ringside view of the accident.

If the Registrar plans to accuse the VC of corruption at the meeting, I'd like to have a ringside seat, please.

Origin The idiom comes from the sport of boxing. The 'ring' refers to a 'boxing ring'. If you are lucky enough to have a seat close to the ring, you can see all the action very clearly.

Roll out the red carpet

Meaning to treat a person like royalty; to give someone a very special welcome.

Examples Raj still expects his in-laws to roll out the red carpet for him.

The fans rolled out the red carpet for the ageing star.

Origin In the old days, whenever the King and Queen stepped out of the palace, a red carpet was spread out for them to walk on. Nowadays, it is rolled out for everyone – Heads of State, actors, sportsmen, etc. There was a time when people thought that the red carpet was "fit only for the feet of gods".

Roll up one's sleeves

Meaning used in informal contexts to mean 'to get ready for a fight or to do some hard work'. It is also possible to say 'roll one's sleeves up'.

Examples When Usha saw the dirty kitchen, she rolled her sleeves up and got busy.

If you want to succeed, you need to roll up your sleeves and take on the world.

Origin — People wearing a full-sleeved shirt usually roll up the sleeves before beginning any work. This is to ensure that the sleeves do not get dirty or wet.

Rub of the green

Meaning — to have everything go your way; to have luck on your side. Mostly used in the context of sports.

Examples — Ananya hasn't had the rub of the green in the last few tournaments.

In order to win the tournament, we need the rub of the green.

Origin — The expression comes from the game of bowls. The players roll a ball on a green lawn. 'Rub' in the expression refers to any obstruction on the grass that changes the course of the ball.

Rule of thumb

Meaning — a method based on experience or instinct, and not on exact calculation.

Examples — A good rule of thumb is to make three chapathis per guest.

As a rule of thumb, do not spend more than two minutes on a problem.

Origin The idiom has been around for over three centuries. When we wish to measure the length or width of an object and we do not have a tape or ruler at hand, we sometimes make use of our thumb to do it. This way of calculating will not give us the exact measurement, only an approximate one.

Rule the roost

Meaning to be in complete control of a situation; to be the decision maker.

Examples I'm not ashamed to say that in my house it's my wife who rules the roost.

Achala may not be the President. But if you ask me, she rules the roost.

Origin The idiom came into being in the 15th century. According to some scholars, the original idiom was 'rule the roast'. A 'roast' is a large piece of meat, and in the old days, it was the master of the household who was in charge of carving it. It was only in the 19th century that 'roast' became 'roost'. This is one theory.

Run the gauntlet

Meaning to be severely criticised by many people; to face or endure a series of problems or threats. The idiom can also be used to mean 'to be attacked from all sides'.

Examples The Minister had to run the gauntlet of angry farmers for attempting to promote hybrid seeds.

Every day, he had to run the gauntlet of hostile journalists and screaming protestors.

Origin The 'gauntlet' in the idiom has nothing to do with the gloves that knights of bygone days wore. The word is a corruption of the Swedish 'gattalope', meaning 'run along a narrow path'. According to historians, when a soldier in King Gustavus Adolphus' army committed a crime, he was asked to strip to his waist and run the gauntlet. The narrow path that he had to run through consisted of two rows of men – in this case, his comrades in arms. As the soldier ran between the rows, the men on both sides flogged him with their whips and stabbed him with their knives. The length of each row was determined by the seriousness of the crime. Very often, the soldier died before he reached the end of the line.

Run with the hare and hunt with the hounds

Meaning trying to be on good terms with two people/ factions that are fighting by supporting both sides. Mostly limited to British English.

Examples Latha is a very clever person. She runs with the hare and hunts with the hounds.

Listen to me, Devi! You have to decide. You can't run with the hare and hunt with the hounds.

Origin Very often, when two people have an argument, they go to a third person to settle it for them. If the person is timid and afraid to take a decision, he will end up saying that both parties are in the right. The individual attempts to be both the hunted (hare) and the hunter (hound).

Sail under false colours

Meaning to try to achieve your goal by deceiving someone; to pretend to be something or someone you are not.

Examples Amrit, the smart cookie, figured out that Hamsa was sailing under false colours.

Vidyashankar claimed to be an expert on the subject. But he was sailing under false colours.

Origin The 'colours' in the expression refers to the flag on a ship. It was standard practice for all ships to display the flag of the country they were from. The only people who did not always follow this rule were pirates. If a pirate wanted to plunder a ship from Spain, he lowered the Jolly Roger (the black pirate flag with a skull and crossbones on it), and hoisted the Spanish flag in its place. This trick of sailing under a false flag enabled him to get close to the Spanish ship. When the two ships were within striking distance, the pirate lowered the Spanish flag and raised the Jolly Roger.

Salad days

Meaning an old-fashioned expression, meaning 'young and relatively inexperienced'.

Examples In his salad days, John fell in love with every girl he met.

The small town hadn't changed much since their salad days.

Origin Shakespeare is believed to have coined this expression in *Antony and Cleopatra*. In the play, Cleopatra says, "My salad days / When I was green in judgement, cold in blood..."

Pronunciation The first syllable rhymes with 'pal' and 'gal', while the vowel in the second sounds like the 'a' in 'china'. The main stress is on the first syllable – '**SA**-lid'.

Saved by the bell

Meaning a difficult or sticky situation suddenly comes to an end before you have to say or do anything.

Examples — The teacher wanted to know who had broken the window. Before we had to answer, his cell phone rang. We were saved by the bell.

Luckily, the guests arrived before I could say anything. Saved by the bell.

Origin — Every round in a boxing match lasts for three minutes, and each round begins and ends with the ringing of a bell. There may be times in a round when a fighter may be doing badly; he may be getting pummelled by his opponent. At times like this, the fighter hopes that before he gets knocked out, the bell rings. If it does, he has been literally 'saved by the bell'. He can go back to his corner, rest and return to fight another round.

Scarce as hen's teeth

Meaning — mostly used in American English to mean 'very rare, perhaps even non-existent'. It is also possible to say 'scarcer than hen's teeth'.

Examples — Recent events have shown that an honest politician is as scarce as hen's teeth.

On the day of the bandh, taxis and autos were scarcer than hen's teeth.

Origin — A hen does not have teeth.

Scot-free

Meaning — to escape a tricky situation without being punished or harmed. The expression carries with it a sense of dissatisfaction, for in your opinion, the individual deserved to be punished.

Examples — Sanjay got away scot-free because people refused to testify against him.

Renu made sure that Jyothi didn't get off scot-free.

Origin — In the past, the word 'scot' was used to refer to what we today call 'tax'. So, in the old days, when you got off 'scot-free', you got off 'tax free'. In other words, you escaped paying your taxes.

Scrimp and save

Meaning — to economise; to spend very little on things in order to save up enough to buy something that you really want – something really expensive. The expression 'pinch and save' has the same meaning.

Examples — Hema and Babu scrimped and saved the entire year in order to go on the cruise.

The young couple scrimped and saved to buy a motorcycle.

Etymology Some believe that the word comes from the Scottish 'scrimp', meaning 'meagre'. When you 'scrimp on something', you attempt to save money by spending less than what is required on it. If a company scrimps on security during times of recession, it is reducing the amount that it normally spends on security – by doing this, it is putting the company at risk.

Seamy side of life

Meaning the unpleasant aspects of life – the violence, dishonesty, crime, poverty, etc.

Examples Raina saw the seamy side of life when he was a social worker.

Jai's new novel explores the seamy side of Bollywood.

Origin According to one theory, the expression comes from the everyday garments that we wear – shirts, trousers, jackets, etc. Compared to the outside, the inside or the underside of a piece of clothing always looks crude and feels rough because of the seams. Another theory is that the seams refer to the underside of a carpet. When a carpet is turned over, all the threads and knots become visible.

Seed money

Meaning: money given to someone to help him start a business or a project.

Examples: Mythreye's uncle was willing to give her one lakh as seed money.

Vishu is planning to start a new business, and he's looking for some seed money.

Separate the sheep from the goats

Meaning: to separate the good from the bad. It is also possible to say, 'sort out the sheep from the goats'. These two expressions have the same meaning as 'to separate the wheat from the chaff'.

Examples: We can't possibly call everyone for the interview. Go through the applications and separate the sheep from the goats.

The qualifying rounds are meant to separate the sheep from the goats.

Origin: The expression comes from the *Bible*. Sheep are often portrayed as being gentle, while goats are shown to be rather unruly.

Set the ball rolling

Meaning — to make a beginning; to do something that starts an activity. It is also possible to say, 'get the ball rolling' and 'start the ball rolling'.

Examples — Ajit set the ball rolling by putting up posters in the nearby supermarkets.

You can get the ball rolling by talking to your classmates.

Origin — According to some scholars, the idiom comes from the world of football – the game starts when the ball is set rolling.

Set/Put the cat among the pigeons

Meaning — to deliberately say or do something that makes a lot of people angry or worried. The idiom is mostly used in British English.

Examples — Tell your students they'll have a test tomorrow. That should set the cat among the pigeons.

The new CEO set the cat among the pigeons when he announced that Diwali would not be a holiday.

Origin — If you were to deliberately put a cat inside a cage full of pigeons, what would be the reaction of the poor birds? They would panic and create a lot of commotion, flying from one part of the cage to the other, in order to keep the cat at 'paw's length'!

Set the Thames on fire

Meaning to achieve far-reaching success; to make a name for oneself. Nowadays, people prefer to say, 'set the world on fire'.

Examples Everyone is talking about Indra's new play. It's really setting the Thames on fire.

We thought that our team would do fairly well in the championship. We certainly didn't expect them to set the world on fire.

Origin Thames is the name of a river in England. Everyone knows that it is impossible to set a river on fire. But if you succeed in doing it, what would be the result? People would start talking about you, and you would become the talk of the town. Some scholars believe that the idiom is a translation of a similar expression in Latin.

Pronunciation The 'th' in 'Thames' is like the 't' in 'ten' and 'test'. The following 'ames' sounds like 'ems' in 'gems'. The word is pronounced '**TEMZ**'.

Shadowboxing

Meaning — when you accuse someone of 'shadowboxing' with a problem, you are implying that he is only pretending to be dealing with it. He is, in your opinion, evading the issue.

Examples — The Chief Minister loves to shadowbox – he never actually tackles a problem.

While the two political parties are busy shadowboxing, unemployment has gone up by another two percent.

Origin — When a fighter shadowboxes, he throws punches at an imaginary opponent. As he is only pretending to be boxing, he merely throws punches into the air.

Shake/Show a leg

Meaning — telling someone to wake up and get out of bed.

Examples — It's nearly 8 o'clock, Remya. It's time to show a leg.

If you don't want to miss your flight, you need to shake a leg, Nitin.

Origin — The idiom has its origins in the British Navy. Before 1840, when rules were fairly lax, sailors were sometimes permitted to take their wife/

girlfriend along with them. While the sailors were expected to report for duty early in the morning, the wife/girlfriend was allowed to sleep on in the quarters down below. To ensure that a lazy sailor was not sleeping downstairs, an officer went down to check. Whenever he came across someone sleeping and he was not really sure if it was a man or a woman under the covers, he used to shout, "Show a leg". The person under the blanket had to stick his/her leg out. If it looked like a lady's leg, she was allowed to go back to sleep.

Shape up or ship out

Meaning — warning someone that if they do not behave/improve, they will be forced to leave; an ultimatum.

Examples — You constantly hand in your assignments late, Nandini. Shape up or ship out.

I am sorry to say that your performance hasn't been up to the mark. Either you shape up or ship out.

Origin — First used in the military during the Second World War as a warning to the enlisted men. If they failed to meet the required standard, they would be sent or 'shipped' back home.

Sheet anchor

Meaning someone or something who/that can be depended on in times of difficulty.

Examples I don't see Dhawan playing the role of a sheet anchor.

Sneha has been Veda's sheet anchor for the past twenty years.

Origin The expression comes from the world of sailing. A sheet anchor was a relatively large anchor that was used only in case of emergencies – for example, when the sea was rough.

Shoot from the hip

Meaning to act impulsively; to say or do things without thinking things through.

Examples As your campaign manager, I strongly advise you to stick to the prepared script. Avoid your tendency to shoot from the hip.

The star became very flustered during the interview and began to shoot from the hip.

Origin To those of us who grew up watching Westerns (cowboy films), the expression brings to mind a duel between two gunfighters. The two men would stand at a certain distance from each other, and the aim was to 'draw' (remove the gun from the holster) and fire as quickly and accurately as possible. The quickest way to achieve this was by firing the gun from the hip – with the gun held low and to one's side. The problem was, it was not possible to be accurate when shooting in this manner.

Short shrift

Meaning — to pay little or no attention to an individual; you show no sympathy at all and try to get rid of him as quickly as possible.

Examples — Rajeevan's proposal was given short shrift by his boss.

Any mention of overburdened students gets short shrift from the Principal.

Origin — In the old days, when the court found a prisoner guilty, he was immediately taken to the gallows to be hanged. Before the noose was placed around his neck, the prisoner was allowed a few seconds to confess his sins to the priest who was present. This brief period in which the prisoner confessed and asked for forgiveness was called 'short shrift'. With the passage of time, 'short shrift' was used to refer to any short period of time.

Shot in the arm

Meaning a stimulus, something that revitalises a person and leaves him feeling a lot better; any form of encouragement that boosts a person's morale. The expression can also be used to refer to 'a drink of liquor'.

Examples The pep talk given by the coach was a real shot in the arm for Ananya.

Winning an Oscar was a shot in the arm for the ailing film studio.

Since I won't be driving, I guess I can have another shot in the arm.

Origin According to some scholars, the expression comes from the world of narcotics. Addicts often inject drugs into their system in order to feel better. The expression was coined in the 1920s.

Shot in the dark

Meaning an American expression, mostly used in informal contexts to mean 'to take a wild guess; to attempt to do something without really knowing much about it'.

Examples When he asked me how I came up with the right answer, I told him that it was a shot in the dark.

There is no negative marking in this test. So, you can afford to take a shot in the dark.

Origin Just as it is extremely difficult to hit a target when it is dark, one cannot hope to answer a particular question or query when one does not know anything about the subject matter. The best that one can do is guess.

Shot your bolt

Meaning unable to complete what one has started; to have used up all one's energy attempting to complete a task.

Examples After the first set, it was obvious to all that Nadal had shot his bolt.

I have shot my bolt, I'm afraid. I can't think of any more ideas.

Origin The 'bolt' in the expression refers to the short, heavy arrow used in a crossbow. Once an archer had shot his 'bolt', he was virtually defenceless because reloading the crossbow was a time-consuming process. The bolt was shot only when the archer was certain of hitting his target. Shakespeare was referring to the arrow when he used the expression in *Henry V*: "A fool's bolt is soon shot."

Sing for one's supper

Meaning to work for one's pay; to do something for someone in order to get something you need or desire.

Examples Ram is in the kitchen fixing the blender. Sita is making him sing for his supper.

Visiting our factories in Delhi and Bombay is part of my job. Like most people you know, I have to sing for my supper.

Origin In the old days, a minstrel or travelling musician used to go from one town to another in order to perform. Very often, he would be invited by the owner of a tavern (pub) to entertain the evening crowd. In exchange for the songs he sang and the poems he recited, the wandering minstrel used to be paid in kind and not in cash – the tavern owner provided him with a hot meal. The minstrel literally sang for his supper. This expression became popular thanks to the nursery rhyme, *Little Tommy Tucker*. According to the rhyme, the poor lad had to 'sing for his supper'.

Sink one's teeth into something

Meaning to bite into something. Figuratively, to undertake to do something; to perform a task enthusiastically.

Examples His new role as a villain gave him something that he could sink/get his teeth into.

The new project is really interesting. Can't wait to sink my teeth into it.

Origin When one sinks one's teeth into a vegetable or fruit, it sometimes requires some amount of physical effort to chew it.

Sit below the salt

Meaning a rather old-fashioned expression, meaning 'a person of very low status; someone whom others generally look down upon'.

Examples As several prominent cricket players turned up for the function, the hockey players sat below the salt.

At the dinner party, Ganpat sat below the salt, with the likes of me.

Origin In the past, when guests were invited to dinner, a relatively large salt shaker was placed in the middle of the long dining table. The most important people among the guests were always seated next to the host. These individuals who were seated at the host's end of the table were considered to be 'above the salt' – in other words, they were people of very high social standing. Guests who were of a lower rank, sat at the lower end of the table; they sat 'below the salt'.

Sit on one's hands

Meaning to choose not to take any action regarding a problem or situation.

Examples As Mala's brother, you need to help her. You can't sit on your hands.

The Government is doing nothing about the water problem. It's been sitting on its hands.

Origin The expression comes from the world of theatre. If the members of the audience sat on their hands in order to keep them warm, the actors would get no applause! The original meaning of the idiom was 'to fail to applaud'.

(at) Sixes and sevens

Meaning to be totally confused; an additional meaning is 'disorganised/messy'.

Examples When the Management changed, we were at sixes and sevens for a week.

Preetam has been at sixes and sevens since the death of her son.

We moved in last week. Everything is at sixes and sevens in the apartment.

Origin In 14th century England, all the companies in the city of London took part in a yearly procession;

the order in which they appeared in the event was determined by the year the company had been set up. Two companies – Merchant Taylors and Skinners – had been established at about the same time, and the parade organisers were unable to decide which company was to go sixth and which seventh. The matter was placed before the Mayor, and he determined that the two companies would alternate. The company that went sixth one year would go seventh the following year. This is one theory. Some others believe that the expression comes from the world of gambling – playing dice.

Skeleton in the cupboard/closet

Meaning an embarassing or a dark secret from the past that one hopes will remain hidden. Americans tend to say 'closet' instead of 'cupboard'.

Examples When the press started snooping around, they found several skeletons in the CM's cupboard/closet.

Dilip is no saint. I'm sure he has several skeletons in the closet.

Origin Many believe that the idiom is the result of something that practicing doctors actually did in the 17th and 18th centuries – hide a human skeleton at home. Before the 19th century, the only body that a doctor was allowed to cut open was that of a dead prisoner. In order to study human anatomy, some unscrupulous doctors hired grave robbers to steal recently buried bodies for them. Once the dissection had been done, they proceeded to store the skeleton in a cupboard. Soon, people started suspecting that all doctors had a skeleton in their cupboard!

Skin of one's teeth

Meaning — to just manage to do something; to achieve something by the narrowest of margins.

Examples — Narsimha got through his maths exam by the skin of his teeth.

We thought we would miss the train. But we caught it by the skin of our teeth.

Origin — It comes from the *Bible*. Job is the man who is believed to have first made use of it: "I am escaped with the skin of my teeth."

Sleep tight

Meaning — to sleep well/soundly. The complete saying is "Good night. Sleep tight. Wake up bright in the morning light, and do what's right with all your might." Some people say, "Good night, sleep tight. Don't let the bed bugs bite."

Examples You've had a long day, Ratan. Good night and sleep tight.

How can anyone sleep tight with all that traffic noise?

Origin In the old days, only the frame of the bed was made of wood. The middle portion – on which a person actually lay down – consisted of strings. If these strings were not strung tightly around the frame, the bed sagged. As there was no support for the back, the person got little or no sleep. When the strings were tightly strung, the bed remained firm, and the person lying on it got a good night's sleep. So when you say 'sleep tight', what you are actually saying is, "I hope your cot is tightly strung".

Smell blood

Meaning to make use of your opponent's weakness or problems to your advantage.

Examples When our main bowler was injured, the opposition began to smell/scent blood.

The Opposition smelt blood and accused the PM of ignoring the problems of the farmers.

Origin When a shark smells blood, it goes into a frenzy. It locates its prey by making use of its amazing senses, and when it finds the wounded animal, it attacks. The wounded animal is at a disadvantage, and the shark makes use of this weakness to kill it.

Smoke and mirrors

Meaning a trick employed by someone to deceive or confuse people; a distortion of the truth.

Examples Smoke and mirrors made the stock market look healthier than it actually was.

Through the judicious use of smoke and mirrors, Mayank tricked many people into investing in his company.

Origin When a magician performs his tricks on stage, he often makes use of smoke and mirrors to make the impossible appear possible; he uses smoke to divert the audience's attention.

Snake in the grass

Meaning someone who cannot be relied on/trusted; a treacherous individual.

Examples Vinay turned out to be a snake in the grass. He used all my ideas to impress our boss.

I don't know why Mrinali continues to trust that snake in the grass.

Origin The expression was coined centuries ago by the Roman poet, Virgil.

Son of a gun

Meaning mainly used in American English to express very different emotions – surprise, shock, joy, etc. Can be used as a term of endearment and as a term of abuse.

Examples That son of a gun actually told the boss to go jump in a lake.

Anand, that son of a gun, still hasn't returned my money.

The son of a gun won the championship!

Origin In the old days, it was standard practice for women to accompany sailors on long voyages. Babies were often delivered on the ship. The delivery normally took place next to the cannons. Since all deaths and births had to be recorded, the newborn's details were written up as well. If it was unclear who the father was, then next to the father's name, the word 'gun' was written – referring to the cannon next to which the child was born. Against the child's name, the word 'son' was written!

Spick and span

Meaning to be spotlessly clean.

Examples I am told that Rama's kitchen is always spick and span.

By the time our parents returned, we made sure the house was spick and span.

Origin The original expression was 'spick and span new', and it was mainly used to refer to objects that were brand new. According to some scholars, 'spick' refers to the 'spike-nail' used in the building of ships. The word 'span' means 'a piece of wood'. So in the old days, when you talked about a 'spick and span ship', you were actually talking about the new nails and wood used to build the ship. In a new ship, everything – the wooden floor, the nails, the sails, etc. – is always shiny and clean. As time went by, 'new' was dropped and the expression was shortened to 'spick and span'. This lead to a shift in emphasis from the newness of the object to the qualities associated with new things – tidiness, freshness, etc.

Square meal

Meaning a nutritious meal; one which satisfies a person's hunger.

Examples Ashwin believes we should have three square meals a day.

You look exhausted. Have a square meal and go to bed.

Origin In the 18th century, conditions on ships were terrible – sailors were given very little to eat. Breakfast and lunch consisted of a few slices of bread and a beverage. Dinner, however, was something more substantial; it was served on a tray and included meat and a few other items. Guess what the shape of the tray was? Yes, it was square. Hence the expression, 'square meal'. This is one of the theories going around.

Stalking horse

Meaning something that is used to disguise one's true intention or objective. The idiom is used quite frequently in politics and business.

Example The party leader wanted me to play the stalking horse.

Origin In the past, when people went hunting for birds, they took a well-trained horse with them. They did this because they found that whenever a solitary horse walked slowly towards the birds, they did not fly away. The hunter walked alongside the animal, and ensured he stayed out of sight by keeping low. When he was within range of the prey, he came out of hiding, and proceeded to kill the birds. In this case, the horse was not doing the stalking; it was merely used as a decoy to divert the attention of the birds. A candidate who is put forward by a party in order to split the opposition is often referred to as a 'stalking horse'.

Stand and deliver

Meaning — to be forced to hand over your money and other valuables to someone else; to be robbed. The expression is considered old fashioned.

Examples — Our coach suddenly stopped, and we heard a man shout, "Stand and deliver".

Stand and deliver. If you don't, I'll have to shoot you.

Origin — This was the expression used by highwaymen (robbers) in England in the 17th century. When these robbers held up stagecoaches, they used to shout 'stand and deliver'. By 'stand' what they meant was that they wanted the coach and the people in it to 'stand still'; in other words, not move. 'Deliver' was the order shouted to the passengers to 'deliver' or hand over their money and valuables.

Staring down the barrel

Meaning to be in serious trouble; something bad is likely to happen.

Examples If the market doesn't pick up, our company will be staring down the barrel of bankruptcy.

Our client is planning to sue us. You know that most people get nervous when they stare down the barrel of a lawsuit.

We were looking down the barrel of defeat when we lost our sixth wicket with only 50 runs on the board.

Origin The original expression was 'staring down the barrel of a gun'.

Steal a march on

Meaning to do something before someone else, and as a result, be at an advantage.

Examples We stole a march on our rivals by launching the product a month before they did.

The company plans to steal a march on its competitors by offering the same software at a much lower price.

Origin Comes from the world of medieval warfare. 'March' refers to the distance that an army could cover in a single day, and 'steal' means 'to do something without the other person being aware of it'. In the old days, in order to catch their enemy off guard, Generals used to march their army during the night. By doing this, they very often succeeded in surprising their enemy. They literally 'stole a march' on them.

Steal someone's thunder

Meaning to take credit for something that someone else has done, and in the process, prevent this individual from getting the public recognition that is due to him/her. By doing this, you become the centre of attention, while the person who did the actual work fades into the background.

Examples If you try to steal my thunder, Satish, I'll have you fired.

The Opposition is keen on stealing the PM's political thunder.

Origin A third-rate playwright named John Dennis invented a machine that produced the sound of thunder. Unfortunately for the dramatist, the play he had written flopped; so, not many people had the opportunity to listen to the sound of thunder produced by his machine. A few weeks later, when Dennis went to see Shakespeare's *Macbeth*, he found that the production company was using his invention to produce the sound of thunder. Dennis apparently became was so angry that he shouted, "Damn them!...They will not let my play run, but they steal my thunder!"

Storm in a teacup

Meaning — commotion or uproar over something very trivial or insignificant. Americans tend to say 'tempest in a teapot'.

Examples — The fight that Sujatha and Rosie had wasn't anything serious. It was just a storm in a teacup.

Don't worry about the silly row. It was just a storm in a teacup.

Stormy petrel

Meaning — someone who is a source of trouble; someone whose appearance is an indication of the bad times ahead.

Examples — My superstitious boss regards Renu as a stormy petrel. Whenever she drops in, we make sure that he doesn't see her.

Please do not include a stormy petrel like Ganpat in the team.

Origin — Petrels are small sea birds, and according to sailors, they usually make an appearance just before the arrival of a storm. The birds are seen as an omen of the troubled times ahead.

Pronunciation The first syllable is pronounced like the word 'pet', and the following 'e' is like the 'a' in 'china'. The word is pronounced '**PET**-rel', with the stress on the first syllable. This is how native speakers of English pronounce the word 'petrol' as well.

Straw in the wind

Meaning a sign of things to come; a small hint of what is likely to happen in the future.

Examples There are straws in the wind which suggest that the two companies will go belly up.

The constant bickering is a straw in the wind indicating future problems for the newly married couple.

Origin A straw left in the open will give you information about the direction in which the wind is blowing.

(the) Straw that broke the camel's back

Meaning to have experienced a series of unpleasant/unfortunate events, with the final one leaving the situation unbearable. Your patience has run out, and you are no longer willing to put up with the way things are. It is also possible to say 'the last straw'.

Examples Sriram is always late to office. On Friday, he failed to meet an important client. That was the straw that broke the camel's back. The boss fired him.

Malathi has always been rude to me. But what she said today was the straw that broke the camel's back. I am going to complain about her.

When Shyam didn't bother to come to the family get together, it was the last straw.

Origin A camel can carry only a certain amount of straw on its back. If you keep adding to the amount, the animal will become overloaded. That final straw that makes it impossible for the animal to carry any more is the straw that breaks its back. The idiom has been in use since the mid-1800s. The expression that was in use earlier was 'the last feather that breaks the horse's back'.

Strong-arm tactic

Meaning to force or threaten someone into doing something.

Examples Listen, if you want to reclaim your property, you'll have to resort to strong-arm tactics.

According to this article, the Chief Minister has been resorting to strong-arm methods.

Swan song

Meaning originally, the expression was used to refer to the final performance of a musician or an actor. Nowadays, it is used to refer to the final achievement or public appearance of any individual; the profession to which he belongs is no longer considered important.

Examples According to the legendary actor, last night's performance was his swan song.

The completion of the project is my swan song. I retire at the end of the month.

Origin The expression alludes to the ancient belief that a swan burst into a beautiful song just before it died. Why a swan and not some other bird? In Greek mythology, Apollo (the God of Music and the Sun God) and Aphrodite (the Goddess of Love) considered the swan to be sacred. According to Socrates, the bird broke into a melodious song because it realised that it would soon be in the company of its master, Apollo. Many well-known writers have been called 'swans': Shakespeare was dubbed the 'Swan of Avon', Homer was given the title 'Swan of Meander' and Virgil was called the 'Mantuan Swan'.

Swear like a trooper

Meaning to use abusive or filthy language.

Examples When my boss saw my letter of resignation, he began to swear like a trooper.

Everyone was shocked when Uma walked in swearing like a trooper.

Origin A 'trooper' is a soldier of low rank. Unlike an officer, a trooper has little or no education, and the language he uses in his everyday speech is full of profanity. Therefore, when you 'swear like a trooper', you are being as coarse as a soldier in the English army. It is also possible to say 'swear like a trouper', meaning 'to curse or swear like an actor'!

Sweat like a pig

Meaning mostly used in informal contexts to mean 'to sweat profusely or excessively'.

Examples When I met Usha for the first time, I was so nervous that I sweated like a pig.

By the end of the first set, Naresh was sweating like a pig.

Origin This is an odd expression because pigs do not have sweat glands, and therefore, do not perspire like humans do. According to some scholars, the idiom refers to the 'sweating' that a pig does when it is roasted over fire. When a pig is roasted, fat oozes out, and it is this fat that is referred to in this idiom.

Sweep under the carpet

Meaning — to attempt to hide something embarrassing from others. Instead of dealing with the problem, you try to keep it a secret. It is also possible to say 'sweep something under the mat/rug'.

Meaning — The Government has managed to sweep the cola controversy under the carpet.

The actor tried to sweep the embarrassing incident under the rug.

Origin — What is it that lazy people normally do when they are asked to clean a carpeted room? They sweep around the carpet, and instead of bending down to collect the dust, they quietly sweep it under the carpet!

Sword of Damocles

Meaning — something bad is going to happen to a person; although it may not happen immediately, just the thought of it causes a lot of worry for the person concerned.

Examples When Govind was told that he had tested positive for HIV, he began to feel that he was living with the sword of Damocles hanging over his head.

Salman lives with the sword of Damocles hanging over his head, knowing that the Mumbai Don is after him.

Origin King Dionysius the Elder ruled over Syracuse in the 4th century BC. Damocles was one of the courtiers in this kingdom, and he spent most of his time flattering the king. Damocles believed that being a king was the easiest thing in the world. In order to teach his courtier a lesson, King Dionysius invited him to a banquet. The food served was delicious and the music played was lovely. Unfortunately, Damocles was unable to enjoy any of these things because unlike the other guests, he found himself seated under a sword – a sword that was hanging by a single horsehair! Damocles was afraid that the hair would snap at any time, resulting in the sword falling on his head. This was Dionysius' way of showing Damocles that although a king is always surrounded by luxury, he has little or no time to really enjoy it. A king's life is very precarious – as precarious as that of the man who has a sword hanging over his head.

(the) Tail wagging the dog

Meaning an American expression normally used to refer to a situation where a minor or insignificant part of something controls the whole.

Examples In some households, the parents do whatever their children want them to. It's a case of the tail wagging the dog.

Instead of following the advice of the Registrar, the VC is listening to someone who joined less than a month ago. It's a case of the tail wagging the dog.

Origin The tail is a very small part of a dog, and usually, it is the dog that wags the tail and not the other way around.

Take a hike

Meaning a slang expression mostly used in informal contexts in American English to mean 'get lost'.

Examples The Chinese have been making too many demands of late. It's about time our Government told them to take a hike.

Some of my cousins were beginning to irritate me. I told them to take a hike.

Take a leaf out of someone's book

Meaning to imitate or copy someone; taking someone as your model and doing the things he does in the hope that you will become like him.

Examples I took a leaf out of Surendran's book and started submitting my assignments on time.

When it comes to discipline, you should take a leaf out of your sister's book.

Origin The word 'leaf' here refers to a page from a book. Therefore, when you take a leaf from someone's book, you are copying what the individual has written. The original meaning of this idiom was therefore 'to plagiarise'. Nowadays, the expression has lost its negative connotation and is used only in a positive sense – 'to imitate someone'.

Take potshots at someone/something

Meaning to criticise or make fun of someone or something rather harshly or unexpectedly.

Examples The article takes potshots at some of the Government's new policies.

The Opposition enjoys taking potshots at the Finance Minister.

Origin In British English, the word 'pot' is used as a verb to mean 'to shoot small birds and animals without taking careful aim'. The reason you do not need to aim is because there are so many birds/animals clustered nearby, that if you shoot in their general direction, you are bound to hit something. Hunters took potshots because they wanted to put food on the table; their aim was to fill the cooking pot! The opposite of 'potshot' is 'fair shot' – the kind of shot a 'gentleman hunter' would prefer to take. In this case, the hunter decides which animal he wishes to kill, aims for it, and then shoots. As time went by, the term 'potshot' began to be applied to any sort of blow – physical as well as verbal – that was difficult to avoid.

Take/Bring someone down a peg or two

Meaning to cut someone down to size; to make it clear to someone that he is not as good or as important as he thinks he is.

Examples It's about time that we brought that arrogant Sanjay down a peg or two.

In Australia, many of our star players were taken down a peg or two.

Origin Navy personnel frequently used this expression in the 18th century. In those days, the importance of a ship was determined by how high its colours or flags were flying. These flags or colours were raised or lowered by a system of pegs; the higher the peg to which the flag was attached, the greater the ship's honour. If the flag was tied to the highest peg, it implied that it was a very important ship. So when you bring or take someone down a peg or two, what you are actually doing is lowering or reducing the honour or esteem of that particular individual.

Take something with a grain of salt

Meaning — not believe or be sceptical about some of the information that has been given to you; to have reservations. This idiom has been part of the English language since the mid-17th century.

Examples — Politicians exaggerate. You must take whatever they say with a grain/pinch of salt.

Ganga is a nice girl, but take everything she says with a pinch/grain of salt.

Origin — The idiom is a translation of the Latin 'cum grano salis'. According to some scholars, Pliny the Elder, in his book *Naturalis Historia*, wrote that Pompey (Julius Caesar's son-in-law) had discovered that his enemy, Mathridates, had found the perfect antidote to poison. Pliny said that for this antidote to work effectively, it had to be taken with a pinch of salt! Readers, however, thought that the reference to salt was a tongue-in-cheek remark: something that was not to be taken seriously. Another theory which has been put forward is that the idiom comes from the world of dining: a sprinkling of salt can make something insipid a little more palatable.

Take the mickey out of someone

Meaning — to tease or make fun of an individual by playing a joke on him or by imitating him. The expression is mostly used in British English in informal contexts. It is also possible to say 'take the mick out of someone'.

Examples — If you attempt to take the mickey out of Ram, you'll get into trouble.

Aren't you tired of taking the mickey out of poor Sadhana all the time?

Origin — Scholars believe that the expression is an example of rhyming slang. The original expression was 'to take the piss out of someone'. With the passage of time 'piss' was replaced by 'Mickey Bliss'. Nobody really knows who this Mickey Bliss was; some people believe that the name was used because 'bliss' rhymes with 'piss'. Later, the rhyming element (bliss) was dropped, and what remained was 'take the mickey out of someone'.

Take the wind out of one's sails

Meaning — to dent an individual's confidence by doing or saying something that he does not expect you to.

Examples — Usha was really angry with her husband. But when he came home with flowers and a saree, it took the wind out of her sails.

The unexpected defeat has taken some of the wind out of our team's sails.

Origin — In the old days, ships depended on the wind to get from one place to another. If you robbed a ship that was sailing next to you of the wind, the vessel stalled.

Take up the cudgels for someone

Meaning — to come to the defence of an individual; to argue strongly in favour of someone or something. When you 'take up the cudgels against someone', you fight against him.

Examples — The Union should take up the cudgels for the two men who have been sacked.

Sunil wasn't willing to take up the cudgels for his friend accused of blackmail.

It's about time that we took up the cudgels against crooked politicians.

Origin A 'cudgel' is a club; it is a short, heavy stick that is often used as a weapon.

Pronunciation The first syllable of 'cudgel' rhymes with 'budge', 'nudge' and 'grudge', and the following 'e' is like the 'a' in 'china'. The word is pronounced '**KAJ**-el', with the stress on the first syllable.

Takes two to tango

Meaning when two people find themselves in a bad situation, and you say 'it takes two to tango', you are implying that both individuals are to be blamed for the mess they are in. One person alone cannot be held responsible for their present misfortune. Mostly used in informal contexts.

Examples Don't blame the fight on me, Revathi. It takes two to tango.

Ajit believes Sunitha forced his son to elope with her. But you know what they say – it takes two to tango.

Origin The tango is a dance form that originated in South America; two people are required to perform this rather intricate dance. The expression became popular in the 1950s, thanks to a song by Pearl Bailey.

Talk nineteen to the dozen

Meaning to talk non-stop at a very fast pace. Americans tend to say 'talk a blue streak'.

Examples Gayathri was on the phone talking nineteen to the dozen.

I wasn't able to concentrate on the novel because the man sitting opposite was talking nineteen to the dozen.

Origin No one is really sure about the origin of this rather informal idiom. According to one theory, the expression comes from the world of mining. In the 18th century, when a mine flooded, engines powered by steam were used to pump the water out. To keep these engines running, coal was burnt. A steam engine that was running or going 'nineteen to the dozen' was pumping out 1900 gallons of water while burning 12 bushels of coal.

Talk shop

Meaning to discuss one's work at social gatherings, when it is inappropriate to do so.

Examples Gentleman, let's not ruin our holiday by talking shop.

I don't want to come. You and Arun will be talking shop over dinner.

Talk through one's hat

Meaning mostly used in informal contexts to mean 'to talk nonsense'. When someone talks through his hat, he speaks about matters he knows little or nothing about; he makes ridiculous claims or statements with the utmost confidence. The original meaning of this American expression was 'to lie'.

Examples At the press conference, the Minister, as usual, talked through his hat.

Krishna was talking through his hat. He doesn't know a thing about cricket.

Origin Nobody is really sure about the origin of this idiom. According to some people, the expression was coined around the time Benjamin Harrison ran for the U.S. Presidency. During his campaign, Harrison visited various places wearing his trademark beaver hat. Newspapers often carried cartoons showing that it was the beaver on top of Harrison's head that was doing all the talking. His opponents maintained that Harrison was talking to the public through his hat!

Talk to the hand

Meaning — telling someone to shut up or stop talking. If the person wants to keep talking, he can talk to the hand because you are no longer listening.

Examples — I'm not interested in what you're saying, Anu. If you want to, talk to my hand.

Talk to my hand, will you?

Origin — The original expression was 'talk to the hand because the ears are not listening'. This expression is considered slang.

Testing the waters/water

Meaning — to determine the opinions of others before actually doing what you want to. This is a term that is normally used in politics and business.

Examples — I think we should test the waters before we open a hotel in this part of town.

Bala tested the waters before putting in a formal request for a new computer.

It was clear to everyone that in his speech the Prime Minister was testing the waters.

Origin — Swimmers usually test how cold or warm the water is before they jump into the pool. Americans tend to say 'trial balloon' and 'send out feelers'.

The devil is in the details

Meaning: frequently used to sound a note of caution to someone; warning an individual that if he chooses to overlook the minor details, his attempt to do something will result in failure. The expression is also used to suggest that something that looks simple may not necessarily be so – the steps required to accomplish the task may be complicated.

Examples: Meera thought she could write the instructions in an hour. It took her all day. The devil was in the details.

It's not as easy as it looks. The devil is in the details.

Origin: It comes from the expression, 'God is in the detail'. This was actually a modification of the French novelist, Gustave Flaubert's – 'the good God is in the detail'.

The end justifies the means

Meaning: any method that we adopt is okay as long as the intent is good. It does not really matter if we resort to wrongdoing in order to achieve it.

Examples: If it means chopping down 200 trees in order to build this shopping complex, it doesn't matter. In my opinion, the end justifies the means.

I think what Chethan did was completely wrong. I don't subscribe to the idea that the end justifies the means.

Origin It is a translation of an old Greek expression.

Thereby/Therein hangs a tale

Meaning when you have said something and then follow it up with this expression, what you mean is that there is an interesting story to be told about the incident.

Examples Janaki has eloped with the driver. Thereby hangs a tale.

Vasu has decided to move out of his parents' house, and thereby hangs a tale.

Phyllis didn't get promoted, therein hangs a tale.

Origin The Swan of Avon, William Shakespeare, coined the expression in *As You Like It*.

Thick and fast

Meaning used in informal contexts to suggest that things are coming at you very quickly and in great numbers. Another expression which has the same meaning is 'fast and furious'.

Examples During the press conference, the questions came thick and fast.

Rumours about their divorce were flying thick and fast.

Origin In Old English, both 'thick' and 'fast' meant 'close together'. The idiom suggests that things are coming at you so quickly that they seem to be joined or 'fastened' to each other. Since the flow is uninterrupted, you get little or no time to react.

Thick of things

Meaning used in informal contexts to mean that someone is deeply involved in what he is doing; he is taking an active part in it.

Examples I don't think you should include Abhay. He doesn't like being in the thick of things.

There was a fierce battle going on, and Suresh found himself in the thick of it.

Think on one's feet

Meaning to react to things very quickly, without having time to think about anything.

Examples Rajneesh is known for his ability to think on his feet. I'm sure he'll do well in the interview.

You can't make Dinesh the PRO. He can't think on his feet.

Origin — Anyone who can think on his feet, has the ability to think while he is on the move/go. Unlike many others, he does not need to sit down and think about what he needs to say.

Third degree

Meaning — any sort of lengthy interrogation done in order to extract information from someone; usually associated with a police interrogation.

Examples — When Viji came home very late, her parents gave her the third degree.

Mohan's wife gave him the third degree when she found lipstick on his collar.

Origin — The 'third degree' is actually an expression that was first used in Freemasonry. A Freemason is a member of a worldwide secret society, and his job is to help other members of the society become successful. The highest rank in this secret society is Master Mason, also called 'Third Degree'. In order to become a 'Third Degree', one had to be ready to be questioned by other members; very often, these sessions not only lasted for a long time, but were also very intense in nature. Whether this was true or not, it became fixed in the public's mind that the Third Degree was brutal in nature – something of an ordeal.

Three-dog night

Meaning — used in Australian English to refer to an extremely cold night.

Examples — Take extra blankets. According to the forecast, it's going to be a three-dog night.

According to Jim, last night was a three-dog night.

Origin — Cowboys spend a lot of their time outdoors looking after animals. During cold winter nights when the temperature dips, the men often cuddle up to their dogs to keep warm. When it is slightly cold, they need the body heat of only one animal to keep warm; such a night is referred to as 'one-dog night'. When it becomes extremely cold, the men require three dogs to keep warm. This practice of embracing dogs for body warmth was quite common among the Australian Aborigines.

Three-ring circus

Meaning — too many activities happening at the same time, and as a result, leaving one confused or annoyed.

Examples — I can't study at home. My visiting relatives have turned it into a three-ring circus.

It was a three-ring circus with my wife screaming, her cell phone ringing, and the TV blaring.

Origin The expression comes from the world of entertainment – the circus. The area where the artists perform their acts for the audience is called the 'ring'. In the past, some of the circuses were so big and so grand that they had three acts taking place simultaneously in three different 'rings'. It was left to the spectator to decide which 'ring' he wanted to focus on. The different acts taking place at the same time were often spectacular, and left the spectator wondering where to look.

Three sheets in the wind

Meaning old-fashioned expression, meaning 'intoxicated or drunk'. Nowadays, people tend to say 'three sheets to the wind'.

Examples Don't pay any attention to her. She is three sheets in/to the wind.

The Captain was surprised that most sailors returning from shore leave were not three sheets to the wind.

Origin The 'sheets' in the idiom have nothing to do with the sheets we normally use to cover a bed; they do not refer to the sails of a ship either. The 'sheets' in question are the ropes or the 'lines' that are usually attached to the bottom corner of a sail.

These lines played an important role in keeping the sails in place. If all the 'sheets' were loose, then the sails fluttered about in the wind, causing the boat/ship to 'wallow': the vessel rolled from side to side, making it difficult for those on deck to maintain their balance. This movement reminded the crew of the erratic manner in which a drunken sailor moved when returning from shore leave. A sailor who was tipsy and not really drunk was said to be 'one sheet in the wind'!

Throw in the sponge/towel

Meaning — to admit defeat and decide to give up what you have been doing; to realise that you will not succeed in what you are attempting to do.

Examples — The odds are stacked against her, but Kshema is not ready to throw in the sponge as yet.

I have a feeling that two of the candidates are ready to throw in the towel.

Origin — This idiom, which is mostly used in informal contexts, comes from the world of boxing. In the past, trainers and managers used a sponge to wipe the sweat off a boxer's face and body. If, during a round, a manager found that his boxer was taking too much of a beating, he ended the fight by throwing the sponge/towel into the ring. This act was a signal to the referee that the manager was conceding.

Throw the baby out with the bathwater

Meaning — cautioning someone not to discard the good things with the bad.

Examples — By firing everyone in his department, Nihal has chosen to throw the baby out with the bathwater.

I don't think you need to change everything, Prema. There's no need for you to throw the baby out with the bathwater.

Throw the book at someone

Meaning — to punish someone rather severely for having done something unlawful. Nowadays, the idiom is used to mean 'to scold or reprimand someone severely'.

Examples — When the student failed to submit his assignment, Prahlad threw the book at him.

As expected, the Judge chose not to throw the book at the DIG's son.

Origin — The book, in this case, is the book of law, and the person throwing it is a learned judge or magistrate. Using the book, a judge levelled as many charges as possible against an offender. He did this in order to impose the maximum punishment for the crime committed.

Throw/Toss the hat into the ring

Meaning — to announce to the world that you are ready to take part in a competition or in the upcoming elections. Nowadays, the expression is mostly used in relation to politics. When someone throws his hat in/into the ring, he is announcing his candidacy.

Examples — Unfortunately, it's only people with little or no integrity who are throwing their hat into/in the ring.

Why don't you make things interesting by tossing your hat into the ring?

Origin — The expression comes from the sport of boxing. In the old days, when a man threw his hat into the boxing ring, it implied that he was challenging the boxer; he was willing to fight him.

Till the cows come home

Meaning — for a very long time; indefinitely long time.

Examples — The two parties debated the issue till the cows came home, but they just couldn't reach an agreement.

You can keep asking for a new laptop till the cows come home, Peter. But you're not going to get one anytime soon.

Origin — Cowherds usually took the cows out for grazing early in the morning, and brought them back in the evening. The original meaning of the idiom was 'entire day'.

Till the fat lady sings

Meaning — a long time from now; anything can happen between now and then. When you say that 'it ain't over till the fat lady sings', what you are suggesting is that you cannot be sure of the result till the very end. Mostly used in American English.

Examples — We thought we had won the championship. But our rivals scored two goals in the final two minutes. You know what they say, it ain't over till the fat lady sings.

Forty runs with one wicket in hand. It's still a possibility. Remember, it's not over till the fat lady sings.

Origin — Richard Wagner, a German composer, always ended his operas with a fat woman singing a solo. According to one story, when a child watching an opera asked his father, "When will the opera end?", he replied, "When the fat lady sings"!

Tilt at windmills

Meaning to fight in vain against someone or something; to battle imaginary beings/things. The expression can also be used to mean 'to waste one's time fighting over trivial issues'.

Examples Trying to root out corruption in politics is tilting at windmills.

The CM would have us believe that we are tilting at windmills. But I think this issue is important. We need to fight it.

Origin The idiom comes from Cervantes' well-known novel, *Don Quixote*. It is about the exploits of an elderly knight and his faithful servant, Sancho Panza, as they travel through the countryside trying to fight injustice. 'Tilt' in this context means 'to joust'; that is, to fight someone with a lance while riding a horse. In the novel, the slightly eccentric Don Quixote thinks that the windmills he sees are hulking giants, and, like any true knight, attempts to slay them with his lance.

Tip of the iceberg

Meaning a major problem; there is more to the problem/ situation than meets the eye. What people are able to see or understand is only a very small part of a big/serious problem.

Examples The gradual downsizing that we see happening in the software industry is only the tip of the iceberg. I think many big companies will fold within a year.

If you ask me, the reported cases of missing girls is only the tip of the iceberg.

Origin We know from the science lessons we did in school that only a very small portion of an iceberg is seen floating above water; the bulk of it remains submerged.

Tip one's hand

Meaning to reveal your plans or intentions; things that you had kept a secret are now shared with another person – either intentionally or unintentionally. It is also possible to say 'show one's hand'.

Examples Ganesh, don't say anything during the first meeting. You don't want to tip your hand.

The star batter refused to tip her hand about her plans for retirement.

Origin The expression comes from the world of cards. When you accidentally tip your hand, you allow the other players to see what cards you are holding – this will give them an advantage.

Toe the line

Meaning to do what is expected of you; to follow the rules and, in general, behave in the way that people in power expect you to. In other words, you conform. The expression 'toe the mark' has more or less the same meaning.

Examples The VC suspended all those who didn't toe her line.

Don't appoint Madhavan. He's unlikely to toe your line.

Origin According to some scholars, the idiom comes from the world of athletics. The 'line' referred to is the starting line of a race. People taking part in a running race are expected to 'toe the line'; in other words, they are expected to keep their toes on the line or behind it. The rules require that their toes are 'on the mark' (line), and not over it. This is just one of the explanations.

Tongue in cheek

Meaning a remark that is meant to be taken as a joke; something that you do not expect your listener to take seriously.

Examples Was Vijay speaking with tongue in cheek when he referred to Sania as the heartthrob of India?

The film takes a tongue-in-cheek look at the world of fashion and music.

Origin To indicate that a comment is not to be taken seriously, the speaker actually thrusts his tongue into his cheek to make it bulge. This is an indication to the listener that the comment is to be taken as a joke.

Too clever by half

Meaning a very annoying individual who imagines himself to be much smarter than he actually is. You are suggesting that he is much too clever for his own good, and this might get him into trouble one day. The expression is mostly used ironically. It is also possible to say 'too smart by half'.

Examples When Prem was in college, he had the reputation of being very arrogant. 'Too smart by half' is how his friends described him.

You should meet the characters in my class. Some of them are too clever by half.

Origin The expression 'by half' means 'very much'.

(have) Too much on my plate

Meaning an informal expression, meaning 'extremely busy'. It is also possible to say, 'have a lot on one's plate'.

Examples Ramesh had a lot of things on his plate. He couldn't go to the party.

When Mala asked if I could help her move, I told her I had too much on my plate.

Tooth and nail

Meaning to fight in a determined manner; to do everything in your power to defeat the opponent. You may have no weapons, but you are willing to scratch the opponent with your nails and bite him, if need be. It is also possible to say, 'to fight tooth and claw'.

Examples The students fought tooth and nail to get the rule changed.

The local residents fought tooth and nail to prevent the Minister from installing a statue of her mother in the park.

Origin Scholars believe the expression comes from the Latin phrase 'toto corpore atque omnibus ungulis', meaning 'with all the body and every nail'. The expression has been a part of the English language since the 16th century.

Touch wood

Meaning when a native speaker talks about the good luck he has had or is having, he usually knocks on or touches a wooden surface and says, 'touch wood'. The expression is mostly used in British English to ward off bad luck. It is said in the hope that the good luck you have had thus far will continue. Americans tend to say, 'knock on wood'.

Examples There have been no protests from the students so far. Touch wood.

The train has been on time this week. Knock on wood.

Origin Some people believe that the 'wood' refers to the wooden cross that people used to wear around their neck. Whenever they were scared, they would touch or hold the cross to ward off evil. Other scholars believe that the expression comes from the ancient belief that spirits lived in trees found in woods and forests. Tapping on these trees was supposed to bring a person good luck.

(to) Treat someone with kid gloves

Meaning to be very tactful; to choose your words carefully so as not to upset the sensitive listener.

Examples Doctor, I need to know the truth. You don't have to treat me with kid gloves.

I think it's about time you stopped treating your students with kid gloves.

Origin The 'kid' in the expression refers to a young goat, and not a small child. I understand that the skin of a 'kid' is extremely soft; in the early 1800s, kid gloves were a symbol of elegance and gentility.

Turn a Nelson's eye

Meaning a relatively old expression that has the same meaning as 'turn a blind eye' to something/ someone. When you turn a blind eye to a problem, you choose to deliberately ignore it; you pretend the problem does not exist.

Examples How can Gautam turn a Nelson's eye to the rampant corruption in his department?

The Vice Chancellor turned a Nelson's eye to the drug problem on campus.

Origin The 'Nelson' in the expression is Horatio Nelson, the inspirational British naval officer who was blind in one eye. In 1801, at Copenhagen, Nelson led the main attack against a fleet of Dutch and Norwegian ships. At the height of battle, Nelson's superior officer, Admiral Hyde Parker, signalled him to withdraw. When Nelson's men saw the signal, they informed him of it. Nelson then took out his telescope and looked through it using his blind eye. He is believed to have said,

"I have only one eye, and I have the right to be blind sometimes. I really do not see the signal." Nelson ordered his men to continue fighting, and a few hours later, after a hard-fought battle, he emerged victorious.

Turn turtle

Meaning anything that flips over or turns upside down is said to have 'turned turtle'. The expression was first used by sailors with reference to a ship or a boat. Nowadays, the expression is used with all modes of transportation – cars, trucks, buses, etc.

Examples Several boats turned turtle during the violent storm.

Raj was killed when his car hit the divider and turned turtle.

Origin According to one theory, when British sailors visited the Caribbean islands, they found that the natives caught huge sea turtles quite easily by turning them upside down. Once a turtle was on its back, it was totally helpless – just like the crew of a ship that has capsized. This explains why another meaning of the idiom is 'vulnerable'.

Twiddle one's thumbs

Meaning to sit around and do nothing; to waste one's time by playing with one's fingers because there is nothing to do.

Examples While my mother went into the supermarket, I waited outside, twiddling my thumbs.

Raghu retires next month. But I don't expect him to sit at home twiddling his thumbs.

Origin To rotate the thumbs round each other, while keeping the other fingers locked or interlaced. No one is really sure about the origin of this idiom. The original meaning of 'twiddle' was 'to be busy about trifles' (things of little importance).

Uncharted waters

Meaning to be in a situation you have never been in before; to experience something new.

Examples You don't expect me to go into uncharted territory, do you?

Being in the final of a Grand Slam tournament is uncharted waters for Andy.

Origin A place that is 'uncharted' has not been explored. As it has not been surveyed, it will not find a place on any map. It is something that is new and never been described.

Uncle Sam

Meaning — frequently used to refer to the American government. Can also be used to refer to the country.

Examples — Why does Uncle Sam keep meddling in our country's affairs?

North Korea is one country that is not scared of Uncle Sam.

Origin — A story doing the rounds is that an ordinary meat inspector by the name of Sam Wilson was responsible for the creation of the term 'Uncle Sam'. This venerable gentleman lived in the United States in the 19th century, and was hired by the U.S. Army to certify the quality of the meat that had been bought by them. Wilson's fellow workers, out of respect for him, made it a habit of calling him 'Uncle Sam'. Whenever he inspected the meat and found it to be of good quality, he put his initials on the container. Instead of scribbling 'SW' (Sam Wilson), he used to write 'US'. When people asked whether the initials 'US' stood for 'United States', Wilson replied that it stood for 'Uncle Sam'! There is, however, little evidence to support this story. The U.S. Army has been making use of Uncle Sam as its spokesperson for many years; most of the posters it uses in its recruitment drives carry a picture of this individual. He is generally shown as an elderly gentleman with a stern look on his face. He has a goatee, and wears a top hat with the stars and stripes of the American flag.

Under a cloud

Meaning — to be suspicious of or have a poor opinion of an individual because you believe that he has done something bad/wrong.

Examples — After working for 20 years, Jagan left the firm under a cloud.

The Police are under a cloud for killing women and children while breaking up a demonstration.

Under the weather

Meaning — to feel unwell. The expression can also be used to refer to one's mental state – to feel sad or depressed about something.

Examples — Shandilya has been under the weather all week.

I feel a little under the weather. I think I am coming down with something.

Atul has been under the weather ever since he lost to Vikram.

Origin The expression has been part of the English language for several hundred years; it comes from the world of sailing. People who go on a cruise often find that the constant rocking motion of the ship makes them violently sick – they keep vomiting all the time. When the weather gets really rough, the ship rocks and sways so violently that people throw up even more. Passengers/Sailors who are unable to cope with the swaying motion are often sent below deck. There are two reasons for this. The first, of course, is that they will be away from the inclement weather; but perhaps much more important is that the swaying motion of the ship is felt far less below.

Underdog

Meaning a competitor who has little or no chance of winning. It can also be used to refer to someone who has no social standing, no money and no political clout. The opposite is 'top dog'. When you refer to a man as being the 'top dog', what you mean is that he is the person in charge; he is the one with power.

Examples We won the game, although we were the underdogs.

As a doctor, I think it's my duty to help the underdog.

You'd better be nice to Ashok. He is the top dog around here.

Origin This is an expression that comes from the sport of dog fighting. In a dog fight, the winner usually ends up on top, while the loser ends up on the ground – under the winner! It is from this that we get our two expressions 'top dog' and 'underdog'. Bookies, who kept a record of how the dogs had fared in previous fights, labelled the two contestants of a fight as the 'top dog' (the one likely to win) and the 'underdog' (the one likely to be beaten).

Up/Raise the ante

Meaning to increase the stake or risk in something; to be in a situation where you are willing to take more risks in order to achieve better results or a better pay off. Nowadays, the expression 'ante up' is frequently used in informal contexts to mean 'to pay up'.

Examples The Union has upped the ante by refusing to meet the Management till all charges against the workers are dropped.

Every time they made him an offer, the star player kept upping the ante.

Sailaja anted up her share of the bill.

Origin

The expression comes from the world of poker – a card game popular among gamblers. The 'ante' (pronounced like the word 'anti') refers to the fixed sum of money each player puts into the pot in order to participate in the game. In poker, all the players are expected to put a certain amount of money on the table before the cards are dealt. Once this has been done, the player who has good cards will increase the stakes by adding more money to the pot – he will 'up' or 'raise' the ante. The expression is used in non-financial contexts as well; for example, in the case of an emotional relationship.

(be) Up to par

Meaning

to meet the required or expected standard. The expression can also be used in the negative.

Examples

My teacher said that the assignment that I had submitted was not up to par. So, she made me redo it.

Most of the candidates who came for the interview were not up to par.

Origin

The expression was first used to refer to one's health. When a sailor said he was up to par, he meant that he should be hired because he was in good health.

Up to snuff

Meaning mostly used in informal contexts to mean 'satisfactory'. Anything that is 'up to snuff' meets the required standard. The idiom is also frequently used in British English to mean 'alert'.

Examples Public transportation in Hyderabad is definitely not up to snuff.

Ramesh was excellent, but the rest of the candidates weren't up to snuff.

Origin In the 14th century, the word 'snuff' was used to refer to the burnt wick of a candle. Later, the word began to be used as a verb to mean 'to extinguish or put out' the flame of a candle. In the mid-17th century, snuff began to refer to the tobacco powder that men frequently inhaled through their nostrils. This process of inhaling something through the nose began to be called 'snuffed'. For several centuries in Europe, taking snuff was common practice among men of a certain social standing. Snuff was expensive, and only the rich could afford it. The common man smoked his tobacco, while the wealthy 'snuffed' theirs. Since the well-to-do were more interested in quality rather than quantity, the expression 'up to snuff' began to mean 'up to the required standard'.

Up with the larks

Meaning to get up very early in the morning. Australians say 'be up with the crows'.

Examples I'm feeling rather sleepy. I was up with the larks this morning.

If you want to be up with the crows, you'd better hit the sack now.

Origin A lark is a bird which starts singing quite early in the morning. Therefore, when you say that you were 'up with the larks', you mean that you got up very early.

Upset the apple cart

Meaning to ruin someone's plans and, in the process, cause problems for the individual.

Examples I don't want to upset the apple cart by asking you to postpone the meeting.

Veeru doesn't take tough decisions because he doesn't want to upset the apple cart.

Origin This is an expression that has been around for several hundred years. The 'apple cart' is the pushcart that vendors use to peddle their fruit. If a cart loaded with fruit were overturned ('upset'), what would be the result? The fruit would get damaged, and the poor vendor would end up incurring a huge loss – leading to his ruin.

Upstage someone

Meaning to succeed in becoming the new centre of attraction; to divert attention from someone towards yourself. The person who was earlier in the spotlight fades into the background. One can upstage someone either intentionally or accidentally.

Examples At the conference, the professor was upstaged by the young scholar.

The veteran actress had been upstaged by a ten-year-old.

Origin The expression comes from the world of theatre. In the old days, the stage was not level; it was designed in such a way that the back portion was slightly raised. This part of the stage, which was slightly elevated, was called 'upstage'. The front, or the area that was closer to the audience, was called 'downstage'. One way an actor ensured that he remained the focus of attention of the audience was to move upstage. This compelled the actors who were downstage to turn around to carry on the conversation with the individual. When they did this, the man who was upstage ended up facing the audience, while those who were downstage had their back to the audience. Since people in general are more interested in the face rather than the back, the actor who was upstage became the centre of attention of the audience.

Wait on someone hand and foot

Meaning attend to the personal needs of an individual; to serve him even though his requests may seem unreasonable.

Examples My cousin Deepa has been spoilt silly. Her mother waits on her hand and foot.

At the new spa, Jyothi was waited on hand and foot. It made her very uncomfortable.

Origin The word 'wait' in the idiom means 'to serve'. Like the modern day 'waiter', the individual is eager to serve the needs of the person he is waiting on.

Waiting in the wings

Meaning ready to be employed; ready to replace or take over for someone.

Examples There are several people waiting in the wings to take over as President.

The players waiting in the wings look forward to the daily practice sessions.

Origin The 'wings' in the expression does not have anything to do with birds or planes. In the world of theatre, the sides of the stage that usually remain hidden by the curtain are called 'wings'. An actor usually waits in the wings before he walks onto the stage to play his role.

Wake up and smell the coffee

Meaning mostly used in informal contexts to tell someone that he should become more aware of what is happening around him; he needs to face the unpleasant reality he has been turning a blind eye to. It has the same meaning as 'get with it'. The expression is mostly used in American English.

Examples You don't know what an iPhone is? Wake up and smell the coffee.

The company is in serious trouble. Wake up and smell the coffee.

Origin Coffee is a beverage that most people drink when they get up from sleep. In the case of this idiom, the individual needs to wake up for he is unable to see what is obvious to most others.

Walk a thin line

Meaning — to perform a balancing act; to be caught between two individuals or groups that have radically different views, and to try to get the job done without annoying or angering either of them. The expression, 'walk a fine line', has the same meaning.

Examples — The Minister knew that he had to walk a fine line between the striking workers and the Management.

Arpita was walking a thin line between being brash and being confident.

Origin — The expression comes from the world of tightrope walking – the skill of walking on thin wire or rope.

Walk in the park

Meaning — something that is very easy to do; something that poses no problems.

Examples — Most students said the chemistry test was a walk in the park.

I painted the kitchen myself. I thought it would be difficult, but it turned out to be a walk in the park.

Walking papers

Meaning to get the sack; to be fired. When your boss gives you your 'walking papers', he is asking you to leave.

Examples The situation is really bad. About fifty people were given their walking papers today.

After Sushmita got her walking papers, she started her own company. I understand she is doing really well.

Wash dirty linen in public

Meaning to discuss in public one's private affairs. Americans tend to say, 'air your dirty laundry in public'.

Examples Political parties are busy washing their dirty linen in public.

In our company, we're told not to air our dirty laundry in public.

Waste not, want not

Meaning if one never wastes anything, one will never be short of it.

Examples My grandmother always reused old envelopes. Waste not, want not is what she used to say.

My father never throws away rubber bands. It's a case of waste not, want not.

Watch grass grow

Meaning a very boring activity.

Examples According to Sujatha, watching people play golf or chess is like watching grass grow.

Usha loved the play. For me, it was like watching grass grow.

Water off a duck's back

Meaning criticism and warnings that seem to have no effect on an individual.

Examples I have scolded Achala several times for being lazy and sloppy – it's just water off a duck's back.

Everyone in my family criticises me. But all that criticism is like water off a duck's back.

Origin Although the duck spends a lot of time in water, the water never stays on its feathers for long. This is because the bird's feathers are coated with oil and this prevents the water from being absorbed. As a result, when the duck steps out of the water, it is able to shake it off within a matter of a few seconds.

Wear one's heart on one's sleeve

Meaning to make your feelings clear to everyone; in other words, you do not hide your emotions. If you are in love with someone, you make it known to everyone that you are crazy about this person. The idiom has been around for several centuries.

Examples It's difficult to know what Asha is thinking. Unlike her brother, she doesn't wear her heart on her sleeve.

We didn't have to ask Rahul who he had a crush on. He was wearing his heart on his sleeve.

Origin During the Middle Ages, when knights fought each other, they would dedicate their performance to a woman of the court – usually someone they were in love with or cared about very much. To let everyone know who the woman was, the knights used to pin onto their sleeve a hanky or a scarf belonging to her.

(to be) Well-heeled

Meaning mostly used in informal contexts to mean 'prosperous or wealthy'. The opposite is 'down at the heels'.

Examples We need to get the backing of some well-heeled individuals to make this project a success.

We should be able to get some money from Javed. His family is well-heeled.

Origin Several theories have been put forward to explain the origin of this idiom. According to one, the 'heel' refers to the heel of a shoe/boot. People from well-to-do families always wear a good pair of shoes/boots and a good pair of socks. Those who are poor, usually walk around in shoes/boots that are worn out. Hence the term, 'down at the heels' to refer to the poor. There is a saying, "You can tell a man by his shoes."

Well-versed in

Meaning to know a great deal about a particular subject. It can also mean 'to be good at something'.

Examples The company is looking for someone who is well-versed in automobile engineering.

Manjula is well-versed in the art of diplomacy.

Origin The word 'versed' in this context means 'acquainted'. Someone who is well-versed in poetry is familiar or acquainted with the subject.

Wet behind the ears/Not dry behind the ears

Meaning someone who is young and inexperienced and, therefore, very gullible.

Examples I wouldn't hire Pankaj if I were you. He is smart, but he is wet behind the ears.

Vani is going into business by herself! Why, she's hardly dry behind the ears.

Look, I want an experienced teacher. I don't want someone who is wet behind the ears.

Origin This is an American expression that has been around for several hundred years. When animals emerge from their mother's womb, they are completely covered in amniotic fluid. Some mothers lick their babies to dry them, while others leave it to the newborns to dry themselves. The last part of the new-born animal to become dry is a small spot behind each ear. When these two spots become dry, it indicates that the animal is a little older and possibly a little wiser.

Wet blanket

Meaning someone who prevents others from enjoying themselves; a killjoy or party pooper.

Examples I never invite Pratibha to any party. She's a wet blanket.

My old boss was fun. The new one is a wet blanket.

Origin For many centuries now, people have used wet blankets to put out fires. When you refer to someone as being a wet blanket, you are suggesting that the individual, like the blanket, smothers the enthusiasm and joy of all those present at a happy event. He dampens everyone's mood.

Wet one's whistle

Meaning: mostly used in informal contexts to mean 'to have a drink' or 'to satisfy one's thirst'. The drink in question is usually of the strong kind – alcohol. It is also possible to say, 'to wet one's beak'.

Examples: Every weekend, I visit the local pub to wet my whistle.

At the end of the day, we meet, discuss politics and wet our whistle/beak.

Origin: This is a relatively old idiom that has been a part of the English language for well over 600 years. According to some scholars, the word 'whistle' in the idiom refers to a person's mouth – particularly, the tongue and the throat. If the tongue and throat are dry, then it becomes impossible for an individual to whistle.

Whale of a time

Meaning: an informal way of saying that you are having a wonderful or a great time; having a blast.

Examples Shekar and Runa had a whale of a time trekking through the woods.

The children had a whale of a time at the party on Friday.

Origin The whale, as everyone knows, is the largest mammal on this planet. The blue whale can sometimes grow to over a hundred feet. Therefore, when you say 'a whale of something', what you mean is 'a large or big amount of something'.

What is sauce for the goose is sauce for the gander

Meaning everyone should be treated the same way; the rules that apply to a girl should apply to a boy as well. The goose and gander in the expression stand for the female and male of the species.

Examples If you're going to punish me for watching too much TV, then you should punish Geetha, too. What's sauce for the goose is sauce for the gander.

If Kishore can submit his project late, then so can I! What's sauce for the goose is sauce for the gander.

Origin The expression comes from the world of cooking – poultry, in particular. The same sauce should be served along with the bird; it does not matter if the bird in question is a male (gander) or a female (goose).

What/Who the dickens

Meaning what/who the hell?

Examples What the dickens were you up to this morning?

Who the dickens do you think you are to give me orders?

Origin The expression has been around for over five centuries. In the old days, people refrained from using words like 'hell', 'devil' and 'Satan' in their speech. It was considered taboo. They felt that if these words were uttered, their souls would immediately go to hell. As a result, they coined euphemisms for these words. 'Dickens' was one of the words they came up with to refer to the Devil.

Wheeler-dealer

Meaning a very crafty person; someone who advances his own cause using unscrupulous means. The word is frequently used with politicians and businessmen.

Examples Well, all the scams we've been reading about show that our wheeler-dealers have stooped to an all-time low.

Anuradha is a straight arrow. She will refuse to join hands with a wheeler-dealer like Sangeeta.

Origin The expression was first used in the United States by car salesmen. When they offered a good price on a car, they called them 'wheel deals'. Since many of the salesmen who offered these 'wheel deals' were not always ethical in the way they conducted their business, customers began to refer to them as 'wheeler-dealers'.

Whipping boy

Meaning a scapegoat; someone who is punished for another person's mistakes.

Examples Poor Raju, he is the whipping boy for the entire office.

Ever since Naila quit, Namratha has become the whipping person.

Origin A 'whipping boy' was usually a boy of ordinary birth who kept a prince company. Like the prince, he was given good food to eat, good clothes to wear, and a good education. Whenever the prince did something wrong, however, it was the whipping boy who was punished. He was the one who received the whipping! Royals couldn't be touched, you see. The term 'whipping person' is slowly replacing 'whipping boy'.

Whistle in the dark

Meaning mostly used in informal contexts in American English to mean 'to make a wild guess'. It can also mean 'to pretend to be brave even though you are scared; to remain optimistic'.

Examples Ramesh had no clue what he was saying. He was merely whistling in the dark.

Harish was just whistling in the dark. He had no idea what was going on.

Shruthi claims that business will be booming next year. I think she's just whistling in the dark.

Origin In order to show others that they are not afraid of the situation they are in, people sometimes whistle. This is their way of showing how 'cool' they are.

Whistle-stop tour

Meaning mostly used in American politics to refer to a brief appearance that a candidate makes in several small towns in a very short period of time. When he visits such places, he makes a short speech, shakes a few hands and moves on. In everyday contexts, the expression means 'to visit several different places – not necessarily small towns – in a short span of time'.

Examples Our candidate plans to make several whistle-stop tours this month.

John and Peter plan to make a whistle-stop tour of India.

Origin In the 18th and 19th centuries in America, most candidates made use of the train to get from one place to another. Whenever a train stopped at a small station, the candidate made a short speech from the train itself and quickly moved on to the next town. Such small stations were called 'whistle stops' because trains only stopped there on request.

White Paper

Meaning a government report on a policy or issue of immediate concern; a report meant to make people understand the issue.

Examples The Minister himself was involved in the drafting of the White Paper.

A White Paper on the future of all Central Universities in our country is expected in a month's time.

Origin The reports are called 'White Paper' because in the past they were always bound in white paper! These reports are generally not very bulky and are made available to the public.

Who is going to bell the cat?

Meaning who is going to perform a dangerous or risky task? Who has the courage to do something daring?

Examples We need to inform the Minister that it's his son who has been leaking information to the media. Who is going to bell the cat?

The VC needs to be told she must give shorter speeches. But who is going to bell the cat?

Origin The expression comes from the world of *Aesop's Fables*. In this particular story, a group of mice hold a meeting about what they can do to prevent the housecat from sneaking up on them. A mouse suggests that if a bell were hung around the cat's neck, then everyone would know where the animal was. The question was, who was going to perform the dangerous task of putting a bell around the cat's neck?

Whole nine yards

Meaning an informal expression, mostly used in American English to mean 'the entire amount, everything'.

Examples For the sake of his daughter, Shyam was willing to go the whole nine yards.

To repay your loan, you have to sell everything – your shares, your car, your house, the whole nine yards.

Origin There are several theories as to the origin of this expression. According to some people, it comes from the world of tailoring – nine yards is the amount of material required to make a decent suit. Others believe that the expression comes from the world of construction. In the United States, sand and cement are sold by the yard. So, when you ask for the whole nine yards, you want everything that a standard cement mixer truck can carry.

Win hands down

Meaning to win very easily, to win without any real effort.

Examples The local team won the tournament hands down.

The media expect Sarita to win the nomination hands down.

Origin The idiom comes from the world of horse racing, and it has been part of the English language since the mid-19th century. Sometimes, as the jockey approaches the finish line, he loosens his hold on the reins. He does this when he is very confident of winning the race; when he thinks that he will win it easily. When the jockey loosens his hold on the reins, he drops his hands. Hence the expression, 'to win hands down'.

Win your spurs

Meaning to achieve something significant, and in the process, earn the respect of others. By succeeding, you prove to yourself and to those around you that you are worthy. People recognise that when it comes to certain activities, you are very skilled. It is also possible to 'earn/get/gain your spurs'.

Examples If you wish to gain your spurs, you need to work a lot harder.

Rajiv felt he had earned his spurs after he made his first million.

Origin 'Spurs' are what one sees cowboys wearing on the heels of their shoes. They are usually made of metal and are rather sharp; a rider uses them to get the horse to do what he wants. Several hundred years ago, even knights wore spurs. While the modern cowboy can walk into any store and buy the spurs of his choice, the ancient knight had to earn or win his. He had to train very hard for many years to become a knight – when he finally became one, he was given the right to wear spurs made of gold. In the past, spurs indicated the rank of an individual. Royalty and knights wore spurs made of gold, esquires wore silver spurs, and commoners wore spurs made of tin.

Win-win situation

Meaning where there is no loser in a dispute/fight; the result is such that both sides get the impression they have won. The two sides are happy with the outcome; each side feels it has emerged victorious.

Examples According to this report, the new proposal is a win-win situation for both seller and buyer.

It is important that you come up with a win-win situation.

Windfall

Meaning a sum of money that you win or receive from someone rather unexpectedly. It is a sudden stroke of good luck. Fruit that falls from a tree because of heavy wind can also be called 'windfall(s)'.

Examples When Gayathri visited her uncle after her marriage, she got a windfall of Rs. 75, 000.

Sameer's garden was covered with windfalls.

Origin In the old days in England, landowners were not allowed to cut down trees which were on their property. The law stipulated that all trees were the property of the Royal Navy, and the wood was to be used in the building of ships. If, however, heavy wind made a tree fall, the 'windfall' became the owner's property. Since such 'windfall' was not common, the word began to mean 'unexpected good fortune'.

Window dressing

Meaning used disapprovingly to mean that an individual is trying to create a good impression by presenting facts in such a way that only the good is highlighted. A true picture of what happened or is happening is never presented.

Examples The Chairman's speech on projected profits for the quarter was just window dressing.

The Finance Minister's article on the state of the economy is little more than window dressing.

Origin Shopkeepers usually have an attractive display of various items in their shop window.

Wing and a prayer

Meaning hopeful, but not really confident, about achieving something; to rely on luck rather than skill.

Examples As he looked at the pitch, he knew that he would have to bat on it on a wing and a prayer.

Raju is taking the interview on a wing and a prayer.

Origin The expression became popular during the First World War. The story goes that a pilot managed to land his plane successfully, even though one of his wings had been badly damaged. When his friends asked how he had managed to land his badly crippled plane, the pilot replied that he had prayed all the way. To which one of his fellow pilots quipped, "A wing and a prayer brought you back!"

Wing it

Meaning to give an impromptu speech because you have had no time to prepare. This informal expression has more or less the same meaning as 'off the cuff'.

Examples I'm sorry, I need time to prepare. I can't stand there and just wing it.

Shanthi left her notes at home. In class, she had to wing it.

Origin The expression comes from the world of theatre. The sides of a stage, which cannot be seen by the members of the audience, are called 'wings'.

Actors often wait here before they make their entrance. Sometimes, actors go on stage without really knowing their lines. In such circumstances, they depend on the prompters hiding in the wings to whisper the lines to them. If they cannot hear the prompter, they make up their lines. They wing it!

Wither on the vine

Meaning in everyday contexts, the expression is used to mean 'to waste something because of neglect'. It is also possible to say, 'die on the vine'. If a project withers on the vine, it 'fails to come to fruition'.

Examples I hope Teja makes the Under-19 team. I don't want him to think he's withering on the vine.

The project withered on the vine because the two parties couldn't agree on anything.

Origin If ripe grapes are not plucked or picked at the right time, and instead are left hanging on the vine, they will gradually dry up. They will shrivel or simply 'wither on the vine'.

Wool gathering

Meaning daydreaming, not concentrating on one's work.

Examples The professor's talk was really boring. I found myself wool-gathering.

Divya, your exams start the day after tomorrow. Stop wool-gathering!

Origin This rather old idiom comes from the world of sheep farming. In the old days, when farmers allowed their sheep to graze, they always sent a couple of women or children along with the animals. When sheep grazed, sometimes tufts of wool got caught in the bushes and on the branches of trees. It was the job of the women/ children to gather the wool and hand it over to the farmer. The original 'wool gatherers' were actually gathering wool! Since the job of wool gathering did not require much concentration, it was possible for the individual to let his mind wander – in other words, he could afford to daydream! Hence, the activity of 'wool-gathering' became associated with daydreaming!

Work one's fingers to the bone

Meaning to work extremely hard for a long period of time. The expression 'worn to the bone' has a similar meaning.

Examples I've been working my fingers to the bone trying to get the house ready for the guests.

Sheba knit three sweaters in a week! She must have worn her fingers to the bone.

Origin The person puts in such an effort that he manages to work the skin and flesh off his fingers. There is no skin or flesh left, only bones.

Work like a Trojan

Meaning to work extremely hard.

Examples Rahul is a good person to have on the team. He works like a Trojan.

The volunteers worked like Trojans and renovated the building in a week's time.

Origin The expression is considered rather old fashioned, and is seldom heard nowadays. The Trojans were people who lived in the beautiful city of Troy. They were very hard working and very courageous. When the Greeks invaded their city, they defended it in a determined manner.

(the) Worm has turned

Meaning a mild-mannered person who is constantly picked on by others, retaliates; the passive individual strikes back, grows in confidence and takes control of the situation.

Examples Renu put up with her husband's abuses for several years. But last month, when he started abusing her father, she hit him. The worm turned.

I wouldn't mess with Rajeev, if I were you. He has changed. The worm has turned.

Origin If you keep bullying someone all the time, at some point he will turn on you. Even the most mild-mannered person will put up with only so much. Normally, when you refer to an individual as a 'worm', what you mean is that he is an unpleasant character. But, in this idiom, it is the gentleness or the harmlessness of the creature that you are referring to.

Writing/Handwriting is on the wall

Meaning something disastrous or bad is going to happen; a warning.

Examples When the team lost in the first round of the play-offs, the writing was on the wall for the coach.

Prabhakar saw the handwriting on the wall when the company fired two more people.

Origin The expression comes from the *Bible*. The King of Babylon, Belshazzar, sees a hand mysteriously appear and write a message on a wall. Being unable to decipher the message, he summons Daniel. The wise man tells Belshazzar that the message is a warning from God that the king will soon be overthrown and his kingdom destroyed.

Wrong end of the stick

Meaning — to misunderstand a situation completely; to make the wrong assumption or arrive at an incorrect conclusion about something. The expression is frequently used in informal contexts in American English.

Examples — Janaki got hold of the wrong end of the stick when she saw Ram talking to Rani.

As expected, the Opposition got hold of the wrong end of the stick and blamed the PM for everything.

Origin — There are many conjectures as to what the stick refers to. Some believe it is a walking stick, while others think it is the stick with which the Romans used to wash their backside. The origin of the idiom, however, remains uncertain.

Yellow journalism

Meaning — to present news in a biased manner; to distort the facts. Newspapers that attempt to increase their circulation, not by providing accurate news, but by appealing to the public's curiosity. The term 'yellow journalism' is no longer restricted to newspapers, it includes all other forms of media as well – TV, radio, etc.

Examples Some of the local newspapers are classic examples of yellow journalism.

To get good ratings, most television news channels resort to yellow journalism.

Origin The expression was popularised in the late 19th century in the United States. Two newspapers, *New York World*, owned by Joseph Pulitzer, and *New York Journal,* owned by William Randolph Hearst, were trying to become very popular among the public by printing sensational stories. Both newspapers specialised in muckraking. *New York World* had a popular comic strip called *Hogan's Alley,* in which the character Yellow Kid appeared. Hearst played dirty and got the comic strip's creator, R. F. Outcault, to join his paper. The angry Pulitzer hired another artist and asked him to continue with the Yellow Kid. The competition between the two Yellow Kids led to an all-out war between the papers. There was a court battle over the copyright, and very often, street fights broke out between the delivery boys of the rival newspapers. The fight between Hearst and Pulitzer over Yellow Kid began to symbolise everything that was wrong with American journalism. If the character that appeared in the cartoon strip had been called Green Kid, we would now be talking about green journalism!